To Lindsay,

keep s… d

Follow yo…

WAVES OF CHANGE

How swimming helped me to
push through grief and turn
my dream into reality

CHANTAL MCFEELY

For Robin and our boys

www.SoulsLightSolutions.com

Published in March 2024 by
www.soulslightsolutions.com

ISBN: 978-1-7385721-0-6

Picture acknowledgements
All photographs by Chantal and Eileen

Printed by www.SoulsLightSolutions.com

Contents

Foreword

From Novice Swimmer to Open Water Legend
By Robin Szmidt, Master Swimming, Ayrshire
(known as Robert in my book)

When I first met Chantal she told me her story of her partner Robin's addiction and death - and her wish to find something positive out of the tragedy. Her idea was to take up open water swimming: not just for fitness and wellbeing, but by raising money and to raise awareness for addiction support and charity.

"While Chantal could swim, by her own admission she really wasn't very good at it!"

While it's relatively easy for many people to enter a short, organised, charity swim and to ask family and friends for cash, that wasn't what Chantal had in mind. She wanted to take on a major challenge of sea-swimming and then, who knows what after that. The problem was that while Chantal could swim, by her own admission she really wasn't very good at it! And her experience was limited to the benign facilities of the swimming pool.

"She wanted to take on the major challenge of sea-swimming"

Ask most people to define "a swimmer" and they might tell you about athletes, Olympic medals and bossy training-coaches: together with the smell of chlorine and early morning training sessions.

Until Covid-times, the idea that swimming outdoors, particularly in cold Scottish waters, is at all sensible put you firmly in the category of 'mad'. Covid-times made people look more and more to outdoor activities, and suddenly outdoor swimming became popular; fashionable even.

Open water swimming offered health benefits and perhaps the opportunity to socialise in a way that wasn't possible at that time. Looked at like that, both pool and outdoor swimming can be self-centred activities focusing on your own fitness and achievements. With my own reputation for extreme and competitive swimming she asked me to help her face the challenge. The River Doon, which Robert Burns describes as 'Bonnie Doon', can be anything but on a cold, dreich, morning and that's where we started.

I quickly realised that Chantal literally had a long way to go.

"We didn't tell her that her training group included two Scottish swim-champions and two winners of national-level open water events"

She joined us for her first proper off-shore swim in the shadow of Greenan Castle. Entering the water in perfect calm conditions, we didn't tell her that the group of four included two Scottish national swim-champions and two winners of national-level open water events.

Making sure that she wasn't left behind we shepherded her like a pod of Orcas looking after their young. As we swam against the tide one of the group members said "she'll never make it": hopefully meaning not that we wouldn't get back to shore but that the challenge she faced, and what she wanted to achieve, was beyond her reach. But Chantal did make it that first day and she's done so every day since.

This book is the story of how she overcame many challenges and how she reached out to achieve something extraordinary. She did this not just for her own sense of achievement but to make a difference, with her beaming smile, to those around her and the charities she holds so dear to her heart.

The book makes us all proud of the part we were able to play in her success. And for me, the biggest hope I have is that Chantal's story will inspire other novice swimmers to push themselves, to be the best swimmers they can possibly be, and enjoy the wonderful benefits of swimming no matter where they are.

Introduction

My love affair with swimming really began at a swimming pool in Brighton at an early morning pool session. I entered the water tentatively and attempted to swim breaststroke. An older man approached me and asked if I was trying to do breaststroke and if so would I like some help.

I confirmed that I was and would love some help. He said he was an ex-Olympian and if I came to the pool every morning that by the end, of the week, I would be able to swim 20 lengths!! I was sceptical but agreed to his conditions. I arrived next morning at 6am.I followed his instructions diligently and by the end of the week I was able to swim 20 lengths of breast stroke!

Fast forward thirty years to August 2018 to when I did a retreat on Holy Isle. It is an that island looked after by Buddhist monks and has a very special, peaceful energy. As I looked over towards Arran from the jetty, I thought how amazing it would be to be able to swim off the pier and swim to Lamlash. However, when asked if I wanted to jump into the waters I declined as I felt apprehensive about getting into the deep waters.

In March 2020 I joined a large dip for World Women's Day, where I met some lovely swimmers. Not long after this event, Scotland went into lockdown. Swimming pools closed and so open water swimming became the only viable option for a swim.

I joined some swimming groups online and started to attend some organised swims. I was made to feel welcome and basked not only in the beauty all around me but in the friendship, laughter and camaraderie I encountered.

Many of the friends I encountered when I started open water, have been instrumental in supporting me to achieve my dream of swimming from Holy Isle to Lamlash. Initially I swam for the physical benefits of swimming, but I soon found that there was something quite special about swimming with like-minded people. There was no judgement about how people looked as once in the water we were all just there to enjoy the adventures and benefits of open water swimming.

The change for me came when my soulmate, Robin, died in December 2020. Coming back from Robin's funeral, with tears in my eyes and a deep sense of loss. I had an epiphany, something deep inside me, a voice saying you have to make a difference, you must turn your grief and sorrow into something positive.

An overwhelming feeling of purpose engulfed me and I surrendered to the possibility and opportunities that lay ahead.

This is when the seed of the idea to realise my dream of swimming from Holy Isle – Lamlash and raising money to support those struggling with their mental health began to take shape, even though I had only recently started open water swimming.

The story of how I completed my swim journey from an open water novice swimmer is chronicled in the following journal entries. It charts the training, lessons, advice and incredible friendships I encountered along the way to enable me to complete my 1.3-mile charity sea swim.

My reason for writing these chronicles is to share my experiences and hopefully inspire anyone who has a thought, dream, bucket list or charity they would like to support. I hope my journal encourages you to find the strength to embark on your own personal journey of discovery.

Maps of swim locations

Maps of swim locations

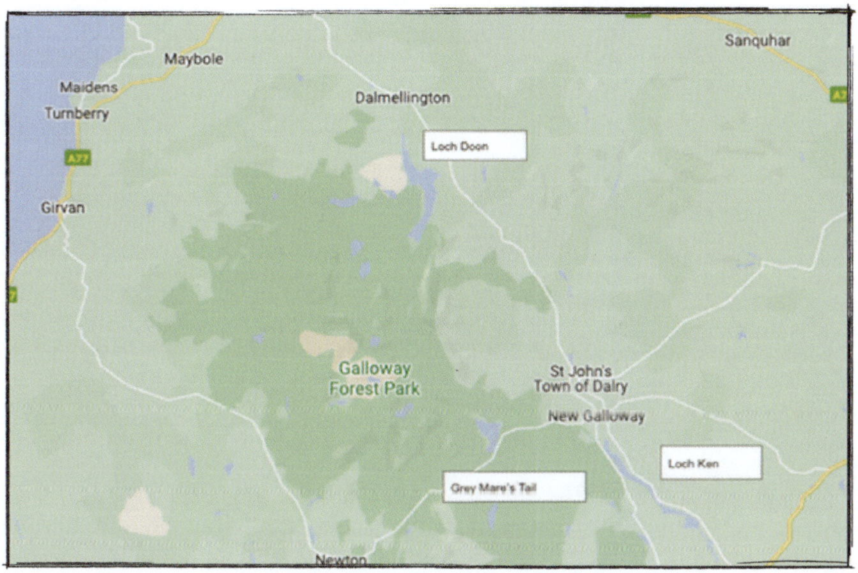

Chapter 1

May 30th - June 28th 2020

30th May 2020 – Barassie Beach

The journey begins!

As I entered the water, I felt a sense of apprehension and joy at finally being back in after three months, the last time being for World Women's Day. I found a safe place to leave my keys by a piece of wood where a couple were sitting, and they agreed to look after them. I put my swimming hat on and was enlivened by the water going up my back through my costume. I then launched myself towards Arran as the sun's rays calmed me and I started to swim. I had been given tips about my arms and how to enter the water for front crawl. I tried to take this all on board, but it was a lot, so I was treading water and resting on my back. After 30 minutes in the water, I felt a pain in my right leg as I realised, I had severe cramps in my calf. I shouted out "ah I have cramp" and then I got really scared. I was used to cramp but not leg cramp. I did not know what to do. It took at least five minutes for it to slightly subside. I let my swim buddies, Ruth, a strong woman who thinks outside the box and inspires me and Linda, who is very motherly and chatty, know. I swam for a bit, but it had knocked my confidence and I said I was going back.

I walked back to the shoreline and then into the car. As I took off my wetsuit and went into the hot shower, I reflected on how amazing it felt and praised myself for doing it, despite the leg cramps.

31st May 2020 – Barassie Beach

"what I would previously have seen as criticism… helped me to grow"

I knew we were meeting at 7:30pm but I wanted to be there for 7:20pm, to be sure. As I arrived outside the chippy, I saw a message from Ruth saying she was going to be there at eight. I was sweltering in my car when my best friend, Chummy, called me and I was happy to have her company until 7:55pm. When I went into the sea, I left my belongings minus my phone and saw a person with a wetsuit and hat, who I thought was Ruth, but it was a man. Then as I looked in the opposite direction, I saw someone coming on to the beach with a pink float and a pink hat. I knew it was Ruth. I walked/swam to meet her and watched her looking towards Arran, shielding her eyes. As I looked across towards Arran, I felt joy and strength from the rays of the sun. I was feeling mentally strong and determined to stay longer in the water today. Ruth suggested that I relax in the water, take my time, and not swim too fast!

I reflected that as well as having had fish and chips 1 hour before my swim yesterday, I was also pushing myself to keep up with Ruth. As Linda joined us, she told us about her weird experience of collapsing with exhaustion on her couch earlier and she was unsure as to why. She was therefore swimming slowly. I did breaststroke with my head above the water for about 15 minutes, I felt relaxed, chilled, at peace and felt I could have gone on forever. I then tried front crawl whilst Linda observed me and suggested instead of taking a breath after each stroke, that I take three or five strokes before breathing, letting out a bit of water slowly each time. The difference was amazing. On the 20 minutes back with the tide I swam a bit of front crawl and felt much better as I relaxed.

I realised in that moment that what I would previously have seen as criticism was really quite constructive and helped me to improve my technique and grow as a person. As I reached the shallow end I glided, head under the water, to get to the shore quickly. It felt amazing! Linda and Ruth watched me till I got out of the water then I waved and headed up to get my keys. Wow what a swim! I felt regenerated, enlivened and empowered.

"Obstacles can be an opportunity to grow or an obstacle to keep you from growing"

(Wayne Dyer)

20th June 2020 – Ayr Beach

"cold water down our necks and wrists to acclimatise "

I was so excited at the thought of a group swim at Ayr beach. I met Katie, my swim buddy, who is a gentle, radiant altruistic soul who offered lots of advice. She suggested rash vests, new lightweight wetsuits to make breast stroke easier, thick socks along with boots to weigh the feet and stop them bobbing up. The water was perfect. She suggested putting cold water down our necks and wrists to acclimatize and to help gain a sense of confidence. The sense of camaraderie was amazing. Even at 16 degrees with the cold water going down my spine, it felt heavenly with the sun beaming down through the clouds onto the water, looking like diamonds glinting on the sea. My soul felt alive as I looked out to Arran and did a full circle feeling totally at peace. I got into a rhythm swimming and felt energized, enlivened, buzzing and zingy.

A first group swim at Ayr Beach

24th June 2020 – Barassie Beach

Glistening sea sparkling like diamonds. The air temperature was 19 degrees, and it was 17 degrees in the water. I started to feel cramp in my feet but managed to swim breaststroke through it. Despite this I felt energised and at one with the sea. It was so peaceful floating on my back looking up at the abundance of clouds.

28th June 2020 – Ayr Beach

"time seemed to slow down"

Wow! A proper windy day for a swim. Gillian, another swim buddy, who is a dynamic relay channel swimmer, had a go pro camera and we went into the water. She had a target, a sandstone building with railings, which I had passed on my walk, now used as a landmark. I started off well, especially when I could fully immerse myself swimming breaststroke. It felt so freeing, and I felt alive. As I reached the sandstone building time seemed to slow down, it took a long time to get there, and I swallowed a lot of water!! However, as I lay on my back looking up at the sky I was filled with the majesty of the clouds, so foreboding, dark and powerful. I felt its strength. I rode the waves instead of fighting them, despite my nerves. I experienced peace in its vastness.

Chapter 2

3rd July – 31st August 2020

3rd July 2020 – Ayr Beach

Despite being wild and windy I went into the sea with Janet, who is passionate about the community and very supportive. She suggested a rash vest as an extra protective layer. She also used a band across her ears to keep her swim hat in place. For the first time since going back in to swim I did not get cramp and it felt easier to swim. I did have my shoes on which, as they were weighted, helped to keep me more streamlined, however my technique needed to improve. Janet explained that Robert, who teaches the triathlon team at the pool, may be able to help. I started to ride the waves and it made things easier, I started to flow, like I did in the pool. I was swallowing quite a lot of water and Janet advised me just to spit it out. I decided to think about the sea to meditate and as I relaxed, I began to feel more present and from somewhere inside me I heard the words "Navigate the storms and ride the waves."

In doing so I began to see a path clearing on to the water, where, if I kept to it, I did not get so affected by the waves. I saw the word 'trust' as I got out of the sea. I realized I was feeling a bit dizzy as I had been in the water at 12 degrees for 50 minutes and it felt cold.

"Navigate the storms and ride the waves"
(Anon)

12th July 2020 – Bookers Pond

"I looked towards the end of the pond and thought "okay, yes, I will do it"

I met my swim buddies at Bookers and it was lovely to see Janet again. I looked towards the end of the pond and thought "okay, yes, I will do it". I felt such a sense of freedom as I made my way to the far buoy. I was alone for most of it. As I was approaching the buoy, I felt my right foot go into cramp. I put one leg up on the other leg as Linda, my swim buddy, had suggested and chatted to Cate, the caring founder of 'The Aquaducks' swim group that I have joined. The cramp seemed to ease and then I started to feel cramp again as I approached the final buoy and decided to call it a day. The camaraderie with some of the other swimmers was great. As I came back from the far buoy, I got totally disorientated. I was so much quicker coming back but realized that I needed a float.

I saw Janet fold over the edges of her float and clip it in place and then blow the float up. I must try that with mine at home. I felt I had achieved something and felt so proud of myself as it was the furthest I had swum in Bookers.

14th July 2020 – By the Millennium Bridge, Ayr

"I had not cemented the swim in my mind until I mentioned it to Robert!"

I met Robert, the experienced triathlete who turned my understanding of how to swim around, who showed me various wetsuits in his garage. Apparently, the wetsuit I had was a surf suit! He was not impressed! He showed me one of his old suits and advised me to try it and see how I got on with it, whilst he tried to repair mine. We walked down to the river at the end of his street, where the river basin was muddy and splotchy until we got out into the middle. I swam to the bridge, firstly doing breaststroke, which was fine, and then doing front crawl. Robert mentioned the craziness of doing breaststroke Holy Isle to Lamlash. After seeing my front crawl Robert said I had windmill arms and was not putting my head in properly. I was also swimming too fast and not breathing properly. I was, however, not disheartened.

I nearly lost my shoe as I got out of the water, but I was determined to do it. Robert could see my determination and said he would help me with my stroke. He pointed to a far-off tree and noted it was 250m. Lamlash to Holy Isle is roughly 10x that distance. A long way! Robert has done quite a few island swims and suggested I need to build stamina and improve the fluidity of my stroke. I said I had a year to practice. He was impressed that I had swum in waters at 4 degrees and felt I would be okay with the cold spells in the sea. Robert agreed to go out again with me next Monday for a longer period. Perfect, I thought. I will practice on Friday when I am at Ayr India with Janet.

"Never Give Up"
(Winston Churchill)

19th July 2020 – Bookers Pond

I went into Bookers Pond with Cate, swimming to the top, which took 60 minutes, a long time for me. My dreamy, funny son Max was on the bank watching and said he would like to try. I did a lot of breast stroke and some front crawl but I was getting very tired. I found out from Cate that I did 700m. Holy Isle to Lamlash is about 1900m, so 2.5 times around Bookers Pond. I would need to build up my stamina, but I knew I could do it.

Looking up at the sky and feeling the sense of freedom was amazing and very calming. I became so aware of nature around me.

A long swim at Bookers Pond

20th July 2020 – Millennium Bridge, Ayr

My second lesson with Robert went better than last week. He took some video footage of me to help show me where I was going wrong. I focused on breathing, so he advised me to look completely to the opposite side of the bank. This felt so much better, although I still felt tired, particularly going against the current. As we entered the river, we saw a swan and its cygnets in the distance, beautiful and special to see. I needed to tighten my goggles as water was coming in.

23rd July 2020 – Bookers Pond

"brush my hip with my thumb"

I met Janet and Cate in the Bookers car park. Using my float today I swam most of the way up using front crawl, but was aware I was drifting to the right, away from the buoy as I approached my next turn. I started to feel tight. I was mixing strokes both front crawl and breaststroke. I was soon on the home stretch and coming back when I suddenly got cramp in my right foot. I tried to stop it and as Janet joined me, I explained what was happening. She suggested not using my legs to do front crawl. She also suggesting brushing my hip with my thumb, which helped my arms not to windmill and blowing out in the water. This was amazing and I easily managed the last 100m. I will adopt this technique next time. Thanks for your advice, Janet!!

27th July 2020 – Bookers Pond

"push my fingers into the water first "

It had been raining all day with the temperature being 13 degrees, but I was determined to go for a swim. Max decided to come with me in his new wetsuit. He wore my swim shoes and apprehensively went in. At first, he said it was cold but soon acclimatised. I had my float and Max held on to it as I swam around the 4 small buoys.

It was lovely to see and have company. I remembered the technique of thumbs going to my hips and breathing out in the water. My arms felt more comfortable today. Janet further recommended I keep my face quite low and just to the side. This was tricky at first and I sometimes got water in my mouth, and that I pushed my fingers into the water first not my thumbs to avoid damaging my rotator cuff. This made me feel much more confident as I swam much easier, mostly front crawl.

"Where your attention goes, your energy flows"
(Mary Morrissey)

9th August 2020 – Bookers Pond

"rotating my body as if I were on a spit"

It was a beautiful Sunday morning as I met Cate at the pond. Frances, a quiet, gentle soul and Alex, a free spirit who is always there for everyone, were also there. The water was freezing as I felt it on my back and took the plunge. I was determined to do my best today. I remembered Janet's advice to brush my thumbs against my hips as this enables my elbows to be in the right place. I also tried to ensure my middle finger on each hand entered the water first. I also remembered Robert saying to look across to the bank.

When I took a breath before going in Cate mentioned someone who suggested she swim taking regular breaths and breathing out normally in the water. I was processing all this information going to the first buoy and strangely it started to make sense. I felt a massive sense of peace and serenity looking up at the blue sky and the water sparkling in the sunlight. I felt truly grateful. Noticing a swimmer doing front crawl, I managed to keep up with him for a few paces before he sped off.

As I swam down the final stretch of the pond, I remembered Chris, a no-nonsense channel swimmer and open swim teacher, advising rotating my body as if I were on a spit. I realized I didn't need to kick my legs as my arms were doing all the work. It felt very relaxing and fluid. As I approached Cate, she said that I was much faster going around and asked if I was trying to beat the other swimmer. I laughed!! As we left, I started speaking to Alex who mentioned she had started swimming open water because of a monk on Holy Isle. I mentioned about wanting to do the Holy Isle to Lamlash swim after doing my retreat there.

"There will be obstacles. There will be doubters. There will be mistakes, but with hard work there are no limits."

(Michael Phelps)

17th August 2020 – Bookers Pond

We did not swim last Friday as the country was in lockdown. Max and I only had one pair of goggles between us, but it was lovely to see Janet and Cate. Max was very happy to come along and once there was really keen to do the whole circuit. I was unsure at first, but he readily swam breaststroke to the first buoy. Cate suggested I just swim ahead with Max to my left. Max and Cate kept telling me that I was drifting offline, but I was quite disorientated trying to get into a rhythm that was comfortable. When I looked up again, I saw that I was heading towards the reeds. I realised that when I relaxed and went with the flow and breathed out into the water, I was far more comfortable.

I also tried to remind myself about my thumb travelling towards my hip to keep me streamlined and the home straight felt so much calmer. I kept the bank to my right so I would not drift off and did about half of this in one go, only looking up to check on Max. He was doing well and keeping pace with Cate. As I rounded the final buoy, I saw Rachel, a funny, chatty, supportive lifeguard who wears 'out there' hats and we chatted for a bit. I went to the final buoy as Max, Cate and Rachel headed to the bank. Everyone was impressed at how well Max did.

21st August 2020 – Bookers Pond

Max and I went to the pond. Janet discussed safety whilst Rachel agreed to swim with him. They suggested I should go for a swim around the pond whilst Rachel swam around the first three buoys with Max, she said he did really well. I managed to do the full circuit of 750m in 30 mins, stopping only once for a deep breath. I needed to stop from time to time because I was drifting into his lane. I tend to drift to the right when swimming front crawl, possibly because I also breathe to the right. Max is doing so well and becoming so strong.

24th August 2020 – Bookers Pond

Max and I went for a swim and the water sparkled like diamonds. We went around the circuit together. I was feeling much more confident now doing front crawl and flowing much more easily. It was incredible to think back to swimming with Robert, when I could barely swim. Such progress!! I felt I would like to do 1k around the circuit and once around the three buoys.

28th August 2020 – Barassie Beach

"It was quite tiring against the waves but far easier when I went with them"

I was so happy to see Ruth again at Barassie today, after such a long time. I was a bit apprehensive about getting back into the sea as it was quite choppy and sure enough it felt quite difficult. The sea was beautiful however as Cate and I supported each other. It was quite tiring against the waves but far easier when I went with them. Ruth gave me a beautiful card for my business and two beautiful plants. Cate meanwhile showed me a more effective way of taking off my costume. Taking the shoulders down first and then putting on my dry robe made it so much easier to get dressed. In doing so I can pull my vest top up over my legs and arms.

31st August 2020 - Loch Ken

"take magnesium and potassium to help prevent cramps?"

I drove to Cate's house this morning and saw beautiful views of Arran. We then drove together to join about fifty other swimmers in Loch Ken. The views were stunning.

As I entered the water, I felt a bit excited and apprehensive as this was my first organized swim and the distance to the other side of the loch seemed achievable but far away. Cate swam breaststroke and we headed towards the middle of the loch. We were thinking about heading out further when we saw Janet and started swimming breaststroke to chat to her. We got three quarters of the way and started to head back.

I am glad we did as I started to get cramp in my left foot. I swam front crawl and tried to ignore it, but it was really sore, then about 100m from the shore my right foot went into spasm. Janet and Cate suggested I get a boat back, but I was determined I would make it to the shore. Despite the pain I made it back to the shore and as I got out, I was elated I had done it, but I was so sore! We retrieved our clothes and Cate gave me some sweetened Kenco coffee. Janet suggested taking magnesium and potassium to help prevent my cramps.

Chapter 3

3rd September – 29th October 2020

3rd September 2020 – Bookers Pond

"power comes from between the wrist and elbow "

Cate met me in the car park and gave me a huge hug! I was a bit apprehensive after the cramp I experienced the other day. Janet also posted to say it could have been the fact that I had been painting all day beforehand?! It took a while to acclimatize but I did it. Cate came all the way around and up the first strait and kept telling me to come over as I was away over to the right (she said afterwards, maybe because my dominant hand is the right one, so I drift to my right?). The float was also getting in my way to begin with but after a while it was fine. My thoughts were telling me I was feeling fast and strong in the water. The more relaxed the better. The slower I breathed out into the water the better flow I had. I remembered Robert mentioning the power comes from between my wrist and elbow as I pulled it back, so it felt stronger.

8th September 2020 – Bookers Pond

Cate is so positive and supportive. We decided to go around the pond, but I kept drifting off. Cate kept shouting at me, and I found it really hard to begin with. I was cold and not feeling it but once I got to the top buoy I started to flow better and by the time I got to the end buoy I realized I had done the whole length without stopping. I really enjoyed it. Cate and I chatted afterwards, and she gave me a Kenco coffee "fix"!

13th September 2020 – Bookers Pond

I met Janet and Rachel in the car park. I gave them both their equipment back as I had bought a new rash vest which fitted better. I could not find my shoes for the water, so I just had my swim socks. I felt cold before I went in but put lots of Vaseline on my body, especially my neck. I had been chatting to Robert last night about the Holy Isle to Lamlash swim. He gave me good advice about joining groups and going with a boat etc. I managed to go all the way around today without stopping. I drifted quite a lot but managed to do 1000 metres! I only felt cramp at the end. Janet and I had an opportunity to chat afterwards. I recognised that I needed to do my swimming in stages. Janet was mentioning various distance swims, she has done up to one mile. Janet said sea swimming is hard with waves. As I finished the day Janet mentioned my stroke.

I had been putting my thumbs on my hips, but they should have touched my thighs. I will try this next time. Rachel mentioned scooping the water back to get more power and said that I don't move my legs at all!! Janet suggested extra speed if I kicked alternate legs gently. I will experiment next time. An informative session with lots to take in!

13th September 2020 – Bookers Pond

"I realised the current was strong and I was drifting."

Before going swimming today, I met my deaf friend Kat, who won a silver medal in the European Deaf swimming championships. She gave me some hints on how to do front crawl more efficiently, suggesting thumbs from hips to shoulder to head, then into the water, giving power from the forearm (as mentioned previously by Robert). I tried this as I went swimming at Bookers today but couldn't quite manage it. I was not feeling it as I was feeling tired but, I persevered. I realized I was drifting off to the right again. I took a dextrose tablet so no cramp. I still feel I need to improve my stamina. As I was coming down the last stretch I was thinking about the white buoys, imagining it was the dome of a lighthouse with the light coming out of it. I came to and realised the current was strong and I was drifting. I felt a bit alarmed, but I did some breathing and focus exercises and was soon fine. Breathing and being calm, I was happy that I managed to control my breathing, hold a good pace and remain calm. Technique to follow!!

26th September 2020 – Barassie Beach

As I approached Barassie shoreline with Max I could see the incredible sunset and my soul felt alive. The car park looked full, but I managed to find a space. I saw Cate, Janet, Alex and Eileen, who spoils everyone in the group and does great marshmallows on her firepit. We took photos and then entered the sea, swimming out towards the horizon, the waves gently lapping around me. It was incredible to be in the energy of the sunset. I did breaststroke so I could see the beauty around me. I felt calm and a sense of oneness with the sea and my surroundings. Once I had swum far enough out, I looked back towards the shoreline and saw the moon as I lay back on my head, resting on my toe-float. Perfect bliss!! The ebb and flow of the current soothing me. As we started to swim back so I saw Max wearing his purple and pink dressing gown waving at me. Using Cate's tips, I got dressed quickly, drinking my sweet coffee followed by fish and chips.

An energizing sunset at Barassie beach

28th September 2020 – Bookers Pond

As I arrived at Bookers Pond, I was happy to see Cate. The sun shone beautifully as Cate, and I went into the pond. It was perfect! There was no one else there and the pond looked so inviting. Cate and I decided to go all around, and we were saying "oh it's so warm" when it was actually freezing (ha ha)!! We were both so happy with the birds at the side of the pond watching us. After a few minutes of swimming slowly I started to get into the rhythm, but my face felt cold as it entered the freezing water. I focused on the peace and tranquility of the pond and practiced my stroke to make it more fluid. Cate said I had drifted away off to the right and directed me back to the buoy. On the next section I drifted slightly again but this time, although slightly off course, I realized I was ready for the last section. I picked up speed and remembered Robert's instruction on how to do front crawl and the power in my forearms, by turning as if I were on a spit. I felt more centered, and my left side felt stronger, managing a whole circuit of 1000m. I will try to go faster and further next time! Cate and I chatted as we made our way back to the carpark and I saw that she was looking shaky. I went to get a coffee and rich tea biscuits to make her feel better. I was so happy, as was Cate, that she was not alone. We had a big hug and after a while she looked and felt better.

2nd October 2020 – Loch Doon

It was a busy day and I rushed back from Braehead Primary school. It was, however, a lovely sunny day as I drove and parked near Cate. I got out of my work clothes and put on my wetsuit. Janet, Cate, Alex and I headed into the water laughing and talking about old fashioned bathing caps. We headed out and started swimming breaststroke but as I chatted to Janet, I started to feel cramp in my right foot. I stretched it out and hoped it would go away. Telling Janet about it five minutes later, she suggested we head back. I swam for a further few minutes but then felt the cramp in my left foot and then in both!! I lay on my back to ease it out, but it didn't work, so Janet and I swam back to the shore. Janet advised me to eat berries with my porridge before my swim and also to take magnesium and potassium with a banana before I swim. She suggested I should also make soup for lunch with lots of oatcakes and cheese and water.

Cramp scuppers my swim!

3rd October 2020 – Barassie Beach

Ruth and I met at 9.30am. I had porridge, 2 mugs of water, magnesium, and potassium supplements. It was cold this morning but so lovely to see the lights over Arran through the slight mist, which had drifted in on the cold. Ruth suggested we swim to a location point 800m away. I started swimming front crawl with my head out of the water as it was too cold. I was thinking I should wear 2 caps as I saw Ruth was way off in the distance. When I met Ruth back on the beach, I told her about my cramps, and she said we needed to swim quickly back before we got too cold. I certainly felt cold as I stripped off and was so happy to have my gloves and that Ruth had given me 2 heat pads before we went in, which I put in my dry robe. Ruth said she would take a film of me. We chatted over coffee and Milky Ways.

11th October 2020 – Bookers Pond

"I felt the cold and started to shiver"

So great to be back at the pond with Cate, Janet and Eileen. I swam with Eileen. The sun was shining so brightly across my path that I couldn't see and so decided to swim with my face in the water.

The warmth of the sun was amazing, and the path spiraled and shone as if to guide me towards the light. I then swam breaststroke all the way to the end with no cramp, however as I came out, I felt the cold and started to shiver, and Cate gave me her fleece as well as warm coffee as it was hard for me to speak. I had 3 mugs of coffee before getting dressed and feeling better. Lesson learned. I need to take fluids beforehand.

"Where we place our attention is what we attract and desire"
(Raymond Holliwell)

12th October 2020 – Bookers Pond

I swam above the water so as not to get my head cold and was also wearing Cate's warm swim socks. We chatted and had a lovely time swimming around the buoys. The sun lit my path again and it felt so magical. The energy and warmth was just what I needed. As I got out, I felt a slight cramp in my right foot. I need to drink more as well as have my porridge and banana. I also need to have more carbs.

24th October 2020 – Bookers Pond

I went into the water with Cate. It was quiet and felt so peaceful. No one was around as we swam 2.5 times around the small buoys. As we swam, we chatted happily.

28th October 2020 – Bookers Pond

"I need to lessen my time in the water due to the dip in temperature"

It was lovely to go for swim with Cate and Rachel, whom I had not seen for ages. I loved her energy as I chatted to Cate going around the pond. At only 8 degrees it felt much colder. We chatted about everything that was going on in our lives. Our hot drinks were definitely needed, and I also reflected that I need to lessen my time in the water due to the dip in temperature.

29th October 2020 – Bookers Pond

There were three of us, Cate, Rachel and Frances, meeting at the pond today. Cate said she would take a photo and video of me going into the water. I was sightly nervous as I went in. Cate then joined me in the water alongside Rachel and as we started chatting, feeling very relaxed. The water was like a millpond, but I could not put my face in as it was still too cold. I could still feel it on the back of my neck afterwards as we had coffee and a snack.

Chapter 4

6th November – December 2020

6th November 2020 – Barassie Beach

"I looked towards the sky and felt my whole-body relaxing"

As I drove towards Barassie I saw the beautiful, bright sun in front of me. I was so excited, thinking I may take a walk and some beautiful pictures from the beach at Barassie, but sadly by the time I went down to the shoreline the sun had gone behind the clouds. It did however lead to an incredible sunset with a stunning orange and gold horizon, and I swan towards it for around 15 minutes. As I rested my head on my tow float, I looked towards the sky and felt my whole body relaxing and said to Cate and Alex that it felt like heaven. They laughed. As we looked towards the shore I was struck by the incredible view with a different panoramic perspective from the sea to the land. Blissful and at peace. I had a coffee and chat with Lesley and Eileen afterwards. So great for our mental health and wellbeing.

9th November 2020 – Bookers Pond

It was dusk as Cate, Eileen and I arrived and there was one paddle boarder in the pond. It was still cold on my left foot, but it adjusted to the nine degrees quickly. I swam with Cate and we had a good pace as we swam two times around the small circuit. By the time we came out we could not see the bank clearly but luckily, we had a head torch and lights in our toe floats. We changed quickly and had hot coffee in the car park. There was an incredible murmuration of birds, all in unison, that looked like a brain toing and froing.

All the tow floats were lit up and it looked so beautiful…

13th November 2020 – Bookers Pond

A very special moonlight swim!!It was lovely to see Cate and Alex. I could see the birds ahead making incredible synchronous patterns. It was truly beautiful. Rachel arrived and swam around with me. It was so good to have her company. Her husband was on the bank where we could see him and use him as a marker due to the fading light. All the tow floats were lit up and it looked so beautiful.

16th November 2020 – Bookers Pond

It was just Alex and I today. I forgot my towel and Alex gave me her scarf to use instead. We swam around the pond, and it was so beautiful – just like a mill pond with a pink sheen and slight ripples. Such a productive swim and we both had a great session.

26th November 2020 – Bookers Pond

I went to the pond and met Cate. She did not have much time, so she videoed me going into the water for the first time without my wetsuit. It was dark and cold, and I only managed about 50 seconds!

1st December 2020 – Bookers Pond

Such a magical swim with Cate and Eileen. The full moon was out as I entered the water. I felt the rays of the moon on me. The water was still, and the moon guided me all the way around for my 400-metre swim. It felt as though Cate and I were swimming in the path of the moonlight until we got out. As I looked back at the pond the path had disappeared. It felt as though it had been there just for me. Such a profound experience.

"It is not happiness that brings gratitude, but gratitude that brings us happiness"
(Mary Morrissey)

5th December 2020 – Bookers Pond

"A true feeling of camaraderie"

It was so choppy today swimming around the pond. It was hard work as the current was so strong. It felt like I was being slapped in the face. I got dressed really quickly after getting out as it felt so cold. Lesley, an artistic soul who says it as she sees it and keeps people on track made cookies and they were delicious. So good being all together. A true feeling of camaraderie.

7th December 2020 – Ballast Bank

AMAZING SWIM!! I did it! I went into the sea at Ballast Bank and swam without my wetsuit. I was unsure at first, but Cate and Alex went in with their swimming costumes, so I did the same. It was difficult getting to the beach as it was so rocky. The sun was shining brightly, and it was 1.30pm! As I entered, I felt the cold on my body quite quickly. Alex said to practice the Wim Hof breathing technique, so I calmed my breath as I felt pins and needles all over my body. I breathed through it and after a minute it started to ease. The sense of freedom was amazing as I looked out towards Arran. I swam back chatting to a lady about wetsuits that were good for breaststroke and buoyancy.

As I got out, I met Paul, a font of swimming knowledge and an inspiration, who runs the group. I felt great at first but then felt the cold and started to shiver. I changed quickly, glad to have had a caramel wafer and my flask of hot coffee.

A sense of freedom…

9th December 2020 – Bookers Pond

I met up with Cate and Lesley. There was a fisherman sitting in his tent. As I entered the water, I did not feel too bad, even though I did not have my rash vest on! I was alone swimming a lot of the way and then I met Brian, a gem and ever-present swim mentor. We chatted for a bit then I caught up with Cate and Lesley and we all swam towards the shore. I am so happy with my 6mm gloves, my hands felt so warm in the water. As I got out of the water, I was so glad to have my cheap £1.00 gloves to warm me as I dressed. We had Bakewell tarts – delicious!!

10th December 2020 – Bookers Pond

Robin (my soul mate) passed away yesterday!!

In spite of feeling so emotional and still in shock I decided to go to Bookers Pond with Cate for a swim. She gave me the biggest hug which calmed and comforted my soul. It felt so good to swim 400m in six degrees around the pond. As we drank our coffee and ate our chocolate bars in the car park I reflected upon the importance of true friendship

12th December 2020 – Ayr Beach (Ayr India)

"I suddenly felt quite emotional as Robin came back into my thoughts"

I met up with Alex and Cate at Ayr India. Max came along and sat on the sand dunes watching our stuff. We walked into the water as the sun came out. I was in my swimming costume and felt pins and needles as I went in.

Alex was chatting about the seals ahead. They were so cute. I had never swum with seals before. They looked like dogs without the floppy ears.!! They were curious about us, probably wondering why humans were in such cold water. They kept popping under the water and popping back up again. I did my Wim Hof breathing through the cold and acclimatized.

I came out feeling zingy, however as I walked towards my car, I stated to feel cold. I stripped off, shaking. I quickly got changed and realized I had not had enough to eat and drink. I suddenly felt quite emotional as Robin came back into my thoughts. Cate let me sit in her car (heated seats!!) and after lots of coffee I started to feel less shaky. I drove home and lay on my bed with the heated blanket on for an hour until I felt calmer and warmer. I soon felt ok.

"As we face our fears, so they no longer have a hold over us" (Anon)

19th December 2020 – Bookers Pond

I was in two minds this morning as to whether I should get up as I went to sleep late. My alarm went off at 8.15am and I was to meet Cate at 9.00am. I had my cereals and saw a few people had cancelled. I took my flask of coffee and decided to go. The sun was trying to come through the clouds as Lesley, Cate and I went into the water. Eileen joined us and took some photos. It was amazing to be out in the water. It was about 6 degrees but looked so beautiful in the daytime. I chatted to Cate and felt so peaceful. We did 400m and then joined each other. My left foot was a bit cold, but it warmed up as we swam to the bank. It was lovely to chat afterwards, and I felt warmer once we had changed. I said I would make galettes (Belgian waffles) for our Christmas eve dip in the pond. Should be a great night.

24th December 2020 – Bookers Pond

Christmas eve!!! My first night Christmas eve swim. I was so excited about going!! I took my galettes and off I went. It was amazing. We all met in the car park (8 of us!!). As we entered the water it felt cold (6.5 degrees) but so clear and we all swam in convoy with our lights either in our toe floats or on our heads. We did 400m and dressed quickly once we got out of the water. Max was there to eat the food (sausage rolls, mince pies, galettes and hot apple juice from Cate's orchard). Such an amazing sense of community.

Christmas Eve camaraderie

28th December 2020 – Irvine Beach

"respect for the swimming"

I woke up at 9.00am and Cate was due to come for me at 9.50am! I quickly ate my breakfast and got ready. It was lovely to go with Cate in her car and we drove to Irvine beach, where I hadn't been before. We met Lesley, Eileen, Alex and Brian. 6 of us in total. The sun was just coming up and people watching must have thought we were crazy. It was 8.5 degrees, not as cold as it had been. Alex, Brian and Lesley were in skins. The sea was so calm. I swam consistently; however, it was much harder on the way back against the current. I did my gratitude in the water to calm myself as the snow on Goatfell, over on Arran, looked amazing! At the end of our swim a man who was watching said "respect for the swimming" as he had been watching from the shore.

30th December 2020 – Irvine Beach

It was amazing to be back at Irvine beach. The sun was out, and the sea was so calm. I decided to swim with my face in the water. I felt the strength and power within me being submerged and at one with the sea. Max was taking some photos, and it was breathtaking as I looked across at the snow on Arran. The camaraderie was amazing although, again, it was harder swimming on the way back. The car park was busy, so I put my clothes on in the back of Cate's car and got changed whilst eating biscuits and drinking coffee.

"Even though a boat may be in stormy seas, under the water it is still"
(Mary Morrissey)

Chapter 5

1st January – 28th February 2021

1st January 2021!! – Irvine Beach

"if in skins, reduce the time in the water!!"

Wow!! I was excited about my New Year's Day dook and a bit apprehensive. I am happy in my wetsuit so was out of my comfort zone in my swimming costume. The pins and needles were quite intense to begin with but eased after a few minutes as Cate distracted me and suggested I keep moving and swim quickly. I swam to the red box and back. Lesley and Eileen were swimming back whilst Max was taking photos from the shoreline. As I came out of the water, I had numbness over my whole body! I dressed quickly as I was worried about after-drop! I made sure I had my flask of coffee but as I got the top half of me dressed, I started to shiver. I had my best rollneck and fleece but was still really cold. Cate gave me a hot water bottle; Alex gave me a pink fleecy jumper and Rachel gave me her husband's jacket.

After about 15 minutes I started to heat up. I went outside to join everyone but was still feeling the cold. The heater from my car was on the whole time and I started to heat up. Note to self. – if in skins, reduce the time in the water!!

New Years Day Dook

2nd January 2021 – Irvine Beach

"I had a hot water bottle today to heat up my clothes"

The sun was shining. A beautiful day! Brian commented that he had been worried about me the previous day because I turned so pale. I met a friend of mine at the beach today and she said she would like to join our swim group. Rachel gave her a safety briefing. I had a hot water bottle today to heat up my clothes but also swam in my wet suit. The snow was still on Arran and looked beautiful. Rachel joined us for the swim today and it was truly magical.

I felt totally at one with the sea. It was great to have my hot water bottle. So needed to keep my clothes warm. I felt great after my swim today. I have learnt my lesson from yesterday.

6th January 2021 – Irvine Beach

I made sure I had my hot water bottle, chunky jumper and flask but forgot my dry robe. Rachel gave me her jacket and said she would not let me back into the water if I forgot my dry robe in future as it was just too cold. We went out into the water. It was 4pm and already starting to get cold. Rachel was spotting for Cate and Alex, who were in skins. We swam to the red box and back. The sun was shining, and it was glorious. I had been out earlier in the day taking photos at Ayr and Prestwick beaches for my calendar. I mentioned this to Rachel and felt quite excited about it. I felt my feet were cold today which was strange as it was not something I normally feel.

8th January 2021 – Irvine Beach

I got into the water at 3.00pm with Alex, Cate and Rachel. They were all in skins except for me. The sunset was incredible. I felt the light heating me as I swam. The air temperature was -2!! It was lovely chatting to Cate. She mentioned making necklaces out of jasper (red stone) found on the beach. The tide was far out today so everyone got out quickly. I felt fine today. Well prepared. Flask and hot water bottle really helped. I took photos, chatted in the car park, had shortbread, and suggested meeting early at 9.00am next day as it was high tide.
(It was due to be the coldest night in few years at - 5)!!

9th January 2021 – Irvine Beach

It was -4 outside, and I was tempted not to go but I was determined to go swimming. I had my cereals, got into my wet suit and was at Irvine beach for 8.50am! I was the first of our group to arrive and the sun was just rising (beautiful). The clouds were pink and fluffy, and it felt so uplifting. Rachel and Lesley arrived, and we went into the sea. Not such a long walk today!

The sea was choppy, so we did more jumping and a bit of swimming. We only did about 10 minutes as the air temperature was so cold, but it was so invigorating.

"Thoughts held in mind must reproduce after their kind"
(Charles Philmore)

15th January 2021 – Bookers Pond

"Swimming in the ice was so good for the soul"

Ice swimming!! My challenge. I decided to swim today despite the ice. It felt amazing with Rachel, Cate, Lesley, and Alex. It felt freezing and we needed to break the ice. I felt so invigorated and alive. Rachel's words of wisdom – "when you feel really cold, towel dry first, or you will go into shock! Then water bottle and clothes on until you are warm". It was my first time getting changed at the pond. Swimming in the ice was so good for the soul.

21st January 2021 – Bookers Pond

Finally, I got to go swimming! I met Brian and Rachel at the pond. It felt cold, especially my feet. I borrowed Brian's gloves. They were so warm (I need to get myself some!!). As we did our 400m around the two buoys Brian informed us that the water was 4 degrees! So much easier getting changed at the pond.

22nd January 2021 – Irvine Beach

I was desperate to go swimming today as I had been looking at my screen all day. As I drove to the sea, I could feel my energies increasing and began to smile and relax. The clouds looked amazing, slightly pink snow clouds. I got to the beach and Rachel was there waiting for me. I dragged all my clothes down to the beach so that I could change quickly. I remembered to wrap my hot water bottle around my clothes. We started with lots of wave jumping which felt amazing, but I got soaked by a huge wave which took me by surprise. We laughed and started yelling. So much fun! I had a big smile on my face! All my worries and fears drifted away. Although it was 8 degrees the wind was very cold, and the tide was a long way out. I need to get warmer socks and gloves for when I come out of the water as I always take so long to warm up.

"Faith gives life, power and action to the impulse of thought"
(Napoleon Hill)

24th January 2021 – Bookers Pond

"The sun came out and sparkled on the ice"

I was so excited that I was going swimming with my buddies. They were already at the pond. As I approached, I saw Rachel who had just been in and said the water was really chilly.

Cate, Alex, Brian and I entered the pond. The left side was icy but there was a path in the middle. Brian and I swam out. He offered to give me a loan of his balaclava for my head. I said maybe I would try it next time as I don't really like things around my head. The water was like a mill pond and I felt an enormous sense of peace, but my feet felt like blocks of ice!! The sun came out and sparkled on the ice. It was good to chat to Cate and Alex. As we couldn't go around the buoys we went straight up towards the top buoy. I realized how much I had missed going up to the top as I don't often go up there in the summer. We turned around due to my feet being so cold. With the sun now on my face my body relaxed. I got out and it was very cold! I dressed quickly and before I walked back with Cate and Alex for my coffee, I took a photo. It looked so beautiful with the ice giving it such a different perspective.

An icy perspective

28th January 2021 – Bookers Pond

I woke up at 6.50am and met my swim buddies at 7.45am. I arrived and went into the water with Cate. Lesley came out early as she was only in skins. I had my hat on and borrowed Cate's gloves, they were so comfy, and I didn't feel the cold although my feet felt numb with the cold! I spoke to Cate, and we swam to the farthest buoy. As I came out the hot water bottle really helped, as did my banana!!

31st January 2021 – Bookers Pond

I was up at 7.30am and had all my clothes ready. I met Cate at 8.30am and we made our way to the pond. It was -3 degrees in my car!! As we neared the pond we almost turned back because it had frozen at the entrance, but we decided to try and clear it. It felt good as we smashed the ice although my neck and hands felt very cold. We got halfway to the first buoy and decided to swim back through the path we had created but it had already begun to ice back over in the 10 minutes since we cleared it!!

Smashing through the ice!

7th February 2021 – Bookers Pond

I met Brian and Alison, another lifeguard, what an inspirational fraternity, who was energetic and smiley, and we swam around the pond. We did a 563m circuit. Initially it felt really cold on my neck and then moved onto my feet and hands. We all felt our fingertips go very cold, so we decided to head for the bank. Such a good feeling to be back out in nature!

9th February 2021 – Ballast Bank

"My coldest yet in the sea"

It was so great to catch up with Cate and Alex. I was apprehensive as it had been snowing and I hadn't been to Ballast Bank in ages.

We jumped down the wall (to get to the bank). I swam in my wetsuit, Cate and Alex in their skins. I went in off the rocks and it was so beautiful to the see the snow on Arran to my left. I had my new socks and gloves on. My feet felt great, but my fingers were still really cold. The outside temperature was -1 degrees and the sea temperature about 5 degrees. My coldest yet in the sea.

Into the waves at Ballast Bank

12th February 2021 – Irvine Beach

I met Lesley and Eileen today. I was totally ready and excited at the thought of going into the sea. As I went into the water I looked towards the horizon. The sky was clear, and the sun was shining as I felt the cold wash down my front and back (Brr!).

I started swimming but the waves were quite strong and at one point I was completely overpowered by them. This was the first time I'd put a hot water bottle inside my dry robe. As I put it on, I felt lovely and warm. I walked up to the car in just my costume and robe. As I was getting changed, I realised I did not have my trousers, so I had to go home in my dry robe, shoes, socks and swimming costume with the car heater on. It actually felt ok. I felt alive and invigorated.

15th February 2021 – Bookers Pond

Such a momentous swim that came completely out of the blue. I met up with swim buddies Eileen, Lesley and Brian. There was still some ice, but I was so happy to be going in. As I entered, I could feel the chill, so I started swimming immediately. I loved the birds circling above and felt an enormous sense of peace and tranquility as I melted into the beauty of the water. I managed to go round the three buoys but on my return to the bank my fingertips started to feel icy and sore. I was delighted to take my gloves off (I may experiment with 2 pairs in future).

I was so happy to put on my dry robe with my hot water inside and I downed my flask of coffee whilst chatting with Eileen and Lesley in the car park. I felt buzzy. I loved my swim, which really cleared my head.

“Assumption if persisted with will harden into fact”
(Neville Goddard)

16th February 2021 – Croy Shore

"I felt like I was static in the water as I looked over to the castle"

I met up with Cate and Alex at Maybole train station for a mystery swim and followed Cate down a small single-track road just before Culzean Castle, at the end of which was a car park. We parked up and my son Max, who was with me, followed Cate and Alex into the sea. It was such a beautiful, secluded spot between Croy and Culzean. I felt like I was static in the water as I looked over to the castle. I borrowed Cate's gloves as mine were still drying. Max took some great photos, and we changed on the beach. My feet felt uncomfortable on the rocks at the edges of the beach. I had left my top at home so had to just wear my cardigan. We had such a good chat and only just beat the tide.

21st February 2021 - Bookers Pond

"I was proud of myself for doing front crawl and putting my face in the water!"

I met Cate and Alex in the car park. I thought it was quite warm today but as I entered the water, I felt the cold. Cate decided to go to the far buoy. I already knew my challenge for today was to put my face under the water.

I went upwards doing breaststroke but realized I was quite slow. On the way back I decided to do front crawl. It took a while to fully immerse my face but what an incredible feeling! My body was so much more streamlined in the water, and it felt really good. As I approached the first buoy again, I started to feel cramp in my left calf. I was trying to think positively as I approached the bank and listened to Eileen as she suggested I stretch it out. I got dressed and was happy to have my 2 hot water bottles and my flask of coffee to warm me up. I was proud of myself for doing front crawl and putting my face in the water!

24th February 2021 – Bookers Pond

"when doing breaststroke, it is important to point your toes to prevent cramp"

I wasn't sure I would be going swimming today as I had a work meeting, but I felt a strong urge to go. I met Rachel as I went into the water, and we chatted as we swam around the pond. It felt a bit warmer, and the rain came down as we went around the triangle for a second time. I spoke to Brian who mentioned the paddles he had on his hands. He asked if I would like to try them. He coached me on their use and suggested I use them as if I was "scooping" something out of a bowl. I was doing this to the side and realized he meant to scoop in front of me.

I suddenly got into the flow and felt my stroke becoming more fluid. I could feel the correct movement. Brian took the paddles back as he said it was easy to overdo it and injure you shoulder. I continued using the same stroke to the bank and felt great, not tired and still raring to go. I changed on the bank and Brian said to me when doing breaststroke, it is important to point your toes to prevent cramp. Wow – what a day!! To think I wasn't sure I wanted to go!!

"Live today. Let go of your attachment to the past as an excuse for your conditions today"
(Wayne Dyer)

27th February 2021 – Ballast Bank

This was the first time in my swimming costume for some time and I wasn't sure if I was going. As I entered my body went straight into pins and needles and Alex suggested I breath into it and after about a minute I felt zingy. I swam out towards Arran, and I felt so free!! I got out and changed quickly putting on lots of layers, my hot water bottle and my ever-present flask of coffee. It was so lovely meeting up with Alex and Cate.

28th February 2021 – Ballast Bank

"Big lesson – get dressed straight away!!"

Back to Ballast Bank!! The sun was out, and I felt so energized. I swam out and felt the rays shining upon me. I swam with Brian, Cate and Alex. We took quite a few photos and then as I got changed, I started to feel cold. I sat against the wall with 2 hot water bottles, one to my front and one at my back to try and get warmed up. I kept drinking as I felt so shivery. Eventually I stopped shaking. Big lesson – get dressed straight away!!

Chapter 6

4th March – 28th April 2021

4th March 2021 – Bookers Pond

It was lovely to see Cate (just the two of us). The fishermen were on the bank, so we worked around them. It was cold initially, especially down the front of my wetsuit. It was amazing to swim a circuit of the pond. I chatted to Cate and felt refreshed, finishing off with a lovely cup of warm coffee.

12th March 2021 – Bookers Pond

I was so desperate for a swim, not having been in since Sunday. The weather was sunny, and it was great to see everyone. Brian, Cate, Alex and I went twice around the buoys. We sat and ate our Ferrero Rocher and chatted happily. A perfect evening.

14th March 2021 – Bookers Pond

Three days in a row and it felt great to be swimming on Mother's Day. I met Cate and Alison at 4.00pm and tried to fully submerge my face in the water but it was still very cold. I thought I would wait and try next week. I will also wear my swim hat as I want to feel that I am more streamlined. As Alison said, "it's hard to swim in a wetsuit as you keep sinking". I felt very calm today as the water itself was very still and I managed to get into a really good rhythm.

15th March 2021 – Bookers Pond

Four days in a row!! Today was great as I managed two full circuits of the pond. Lovely to be with Cate and Rachel once more. Alison lent me her hat and it did feel warmer with it on.

16th March 2021 – Bookers Pond (again)!!

It was quite choppy today and I met Cate & Alex. I decided to wear two hats with my goggles!! I did three circuits of the pond and really got into a great rhythm when my head was in the water although I did get slight "brain freeze"!!

Alison was instructing me in back-stroke swimming. Arms at five past and five to on the clock with slightly bent arms at the elbow and push!! She seemed to glide through the water, and I thought I may try it next day if Alison is there again.

17th March 2021 – Bookers Pond

Such a beautiful sunset! After taking a while for my feet to warm up yesterday I only swam around the buoys twice. It was lovely to see Rachel. Alex and I swam around together but it was so calming when I swam around, most of the way, on my own. Lesley and Eileen have agreed to go swimming tomorrow.

18th March 2021 – Irvine Beach

Back to Irvine beach!! The sun shone brightly, and Lesley and Eileen were in the water already as I arrived. It was really choppy. I got soaked today but it was so much fun. I loved it!! I took some photos and generally felt very energised.

Choppy waters at sunset

19th March 2021 – Ballast Bank

An impromptu swim today. First day of my period!! I was unsure but decided to go with Cate and Alex at 5.00pm. As I arrived the sun was shining, and the sea looked so inviting. I went into the water in my wetsuit. It was quite choppy but very invigorating. I really didn't want to leave.

There was quite a large swell by the rocks. Alex gave me some new socks and I had some hot coffee from my flask.

22nd March 2021 – Bookers Pond

"Deep inside I decided I wanted to increase my laps"

My first lunchtime swim for a while! I was determined to get out before my evening course. I met Cate, Alison and her son Leigh, Alison's son, a good competitive swimmer. She mentioned that she and Brian used to be swim instructors together. I just did 1 circuit today. It was cold at first and then I watched the ripples of the water as I was swimming, which calmed me and helped me get into the flow. As I was changing on the bank, I looked across the water and saw Alison. Leigh said he was on his fifth lap. Deep inside I decided I wanted to increase my laps.

25th March 2021 – Bookers Pond

"stretching my arms out as far as I could so that I would glide"

Max came with me today as my spotter as I was not sure if anyone would be there, and I was determined to do a circuit. Brian joined Max and I and we did a circuit. He imparted a swim nugget today. He suggested stretching my arms out as far as I could so that I would glide. I will try to practice this tomorrow. Brian's advice reminded me of my first teacher when I was 18 at Prince Regent swimming pool in Brighton. I used to go at 7.00am before work and I tried to do breaststroke.

A man approached me and asked if I wanted help. He explained that he was an ex-Olympian and that if I went at 6.00am every morning he would teach me and by the end of the week I was able to do 20 lengths.

A good intention requires the support of good action in order to translate it into a positive outcome"
(Trishna Damodar)

27th March 2021 – Bookers Pond

I was not sure if I would get a chance to go swimming today as I missed the midday swim. Brian said he was going to the pond at 4.00pm so I decided to join him. He loaned me his goggles as I was determined to put my face in the water. It took me about three quarters of a circuit to finally put my face in. I felt so streamlined and as I approached the bank,

I had my arms outstretched, pulling back and pushing my feet down. As I exited Brian said he was impressed at my speed and positioning of my face in the water. I will wear ear plugs tomorrow as they were feeling a bit uncomfortable. I will try to do 3 circuits next time I come.

28th March 2021 – Bookers Pond

I met Brian at the pond today. As we entered it was colder today at 8.7 degrees and was dreich (cloudy, wet, and damp). Due to it being so cold it took about three quarters of a circuit again to put my face in the water. Once I got used to it the second circuit was amazing, once I had warmed up. I swam towards the shore full pelt, gliding. I felt fit, strong, and alive.

31st March 2021- Bookers Pond

"breaststroke was 70% legs!"

The sun was shining, and I met Brian at the pond again today. It was quite cold and very choppy, and I kept getting slapped in the face and neck. It took me about half a circuit to put my face in the water. On the last section of the first lap Brian said he noticed I was not using my feet much and that breaststroke was 70% legs! He tried to explain but I was getting buffeted by the waves. I tried to close my eyes and go around again, focusing on my feet, but it was tricky. Brian had said to put my feet up to my bum, then out and slap my heels together. He suggested I lie on the bank and moved my legs for me. It felt so strange and not what I had been doing. I was grateful to have been shown how to do it properly.

1st April 2021 – Bookers Pond

Today I managed 4 circuits of the pond (1000m). I was so excited. It really flowed and I felt natural and in alignment today. I felt cold afterwards, and my feet felt numb but also felt an overwhelming sense of peace.

"Self-control is strength.....right thought is mastery.... calmness is power"
(James Allen As a Man Thinketh)

2nd April 2021 – Bookers Pond

I met Brian at the pond today and only did 2 circuits as I felt the force of the current and was practicing my new kicks. It was very tiring, but I really enjoyed it and it made sense. It was busy with kayakers today, possibly because it was Good Friday.

3rd April 2021 – Irvine Beach

"I had swum 1.2km. This brought my dream of swimming from Holy Isle to Lamlash (1.3 miles) slightly closer!!"

I met Alison at 8.30am and as we entered the sea it was like a mill pond. I was going to take a photo and then realized it was the same scene as the front of my photo book!

I was determined to try out my newly improved stroke and push myself. Alison mentioned swimming to the stone dragon, a statue on the hill. I had never noticed it before. As we started swimming towards it the sense of peace was incredible. Once I could put my face into the water, I found a comfortable rhythm. I looked up occasionally to check my bearings and then continued. I felt like I could have swum forever. During one of my checks, I realized I had nearly reached the dragon. The coastline looked different, I looked back to where we had left our clothes and it looked so far away. My mind felt free and so did I. Once we returned to the shore, I was shocked and delighted as Alison informed me that we had swum 1.2km. This brought my dream of swimming from Holy Isle to Lamlash (1.3 miles) slightly closer!!

4th April 2021 – Bookers Pond

"I reflected that it is only 5 months until I undertake my Holy Isle swim"

It was colder at the pond today. I met Lesley and Eileen and as we swam, I felt a huge difference in my speed. I managed 3 circuits before my fingers started to feel cold. After my swim yesterday I reflected that it is only 5 months until I undertake my Holy Isle swim.

As I exited Lesley suggested that I would go further if I stretched more at the end of my stroke. I really appreciated her comments as I just want to improve. I will practice this tomorrow.

5th April 2021 -Bookers Pond

I met Brian, Alison, and Lesley at the pond today, Cate and Eileen were already in. Between the first and second buoy it was so choppy I felt like I was being stopped and lots of water was slapping me in the face, but I kept persevering through it all. I only managed 2 circuits and I practiced my glide (as much as I could with the waves). It was cold coming out, so I warmed up with my hot drink chatting with Brian and Eileen.

"The eye of the storm silent and quiet. Listen to our inner voice"
(Mary Morrissey)

8th April 2021 – Bookers Pond

I was in two minds whether to go or not today as it was so cold. I heated everything up and went. There were 8 of us today. Amazing!! It was very wet but once in the water it was reasonably calm.

I got into my rhythm and consciously focused on my arms today, trying to stretch them out. It seemed to take a long time to get to the first buoy but once my face was in the water I felt more in alignment. I focused on my feet as they were feeling a bit uncomfortable, and I told my feet to relax and not cramp! I stretched out my toes and managed 3 times around. As I got to the bank, I felt a bit disorientated. I started to get changed on the bank, but the rain was too heavy. I ended up going home in my dry robe, which felt quite invigorating, if quite chilly.

9th April 2021 – Bookers Pond

"to stop my neck being sore I could tuck my chin into my chest"

I was meeting everyone today at 11.00am and thought I would be open to trying front crawl. The sun was shining, and the sky was blue, and I was excited to go in. Brian was ahead of me in the water and was doing a circuit. I decided after yesterday's 5 circuits around the pond to try and do a full circuit. I tried to remember all the advice I had been given and as I was swimming towards the bottom of the pond, I saw Brian alongside me. He suggested that to stop my neck being sore I could tuck my chin into my chest as I stretched my arms and legs out to create a more wave-like motion.

I tried this and what a difference, much more streamlined and smoother. Once I came out Brian said that Holy Isle to Lamlash is 1.3 miles and that if I would like to do it, he would kayak alongside me.

"Once you make a decision you will find all the people, resources and ideas that you need"
(Bob Proctor)

12th April 2021 – Bookers Pond

"I had knocked 10/15 minutes off my swim time. Yippee!"

I joined Brian and Alison and decided to swim around the whole pond again. The weather was sunny but there was a chill in the air. It was not until I reached the top buoy that I eventually started to warm up. I took my time and remembered Brian's words "chin to chest and straight arms and legs". As I swam around the second and third buoys I was blinded by the sunlight and found it difficult to see the buoy. At the end of the circuit, I wondered where everyone was. I saw Brian at the bank. He said he was amazed at my performance as I had knocked 10/15 minutes off my time. Yippee!

17th April 2021 - Bookers Pond

I was back at the pond today after my trip to Arran. I met Brian and Alison in the car park. The weather was beautiful, and I decided to swim a full circuit. I realized that it takes me a while to put my face in the water. However, when I do, my swim feels more natural and relaxing. I did a Pacman circuit for the first time today (about 1000m) and would have done a small circuit, but I got cramp in my foot. I think this was because I did not have my banana and I had been rushing around today. Brian said I swam well today, he could not fault me and said he would teach me front crawl, which would be easier than breaststroke for my Lamlash swim. Roll on tomorrow!

18th April 2021 – Bookers Pond

I met Brian in the car park, and he was keen to show me how to swim front crawl. He focused on my arms first and as we reached the first buoy, we did some breathing exercises. He then watched my stroke. He said it was quite good but that I was going to the right because my left arm was coming over my centre line. I practiced this and put my chest to my chin. I will continue with the breathing exercises next time, gradually breathing out into the water.

21st April 2021 – Bookers Pond

I met Brian, Alison, and Leigh today and decided to do a full circuit. As it was still quite cold, I waited until the first buoy to put my face in the water. It felt great to swim at my own pace. Halfway down the home straight I got cramp in my right foot. I continued to the Pacman. I felt cramp in my other foot. Brian stayed with me and stretched out my feet and calves. Alison almost needed to tow me back!

22nd April 2021 – Bookers Pond

I decided to go into the pond today to overcome my fear of cramps. Prior to entering I recorded a video about nature for the Mental Health Foundation, with Max asking questions. I started swimming without any expectations. I headed up to the top of the pond and was joined briefly by Alison and Brian and then I was alone. I loved the sense of peace and being with my thoughts. As I swam back, I felt the slight beginnings of cramp. I really slowed down and stretched out my arms and legs and started to focus on positive thoughts. I had also made sure I had my banana and potassium and magnesium tablets before I went in. I managed a circuit and a triangle. I felt a real sense of achievement. Roll on tomorrow!

23rd April 2021 – Bookers Pond

I felt peaceful as I swam around Bookers Pond. My strokes flowed and I felt at one with the water. I wanted to try 2 circuits today but needed to get back for yoga. I managed a Pacman and a triangle. I would love to go for a midnight swim tomorrow.

24th April 2021 – Barassie Beach

AMAZING!! My dream to swim at night has been realised. I met Eileen and Lesley in the car park at 11.00pm. Lesley let me borrow her nightlight. The tide was in, but we still needed to walk quite far as it was shallow. Once in it was incredible and I did not want to get out. It was as though the moon had put a spell on me. I was captivated and felt alive, energized and at peace. Swimming in the rays of the moon was just bliss!!

My dream to swim at night has been realised

25th April 2021 – Bookers Pond

I was unsure if I wanted to go to the pond, as it had dropped to 10 degrees from 25 degrees, and I felt quite cold. I pushed myself to go and met Brian at the pond. I was feeling quite tired and achy in my joints. As I entered the water it felt cold and seemed to take forever to get to the second buoy and felt like hard work! I had a chat to myself and said I am doing the best I can from the second to the third buoy and started to feel calmer. For the final part of my swim, I imagined that I was swimming from Holy Isle to Lamlash. It felt more natural, fluid and streamlined as I started to do this, and I completed the circuit. As I got out, I had a chat with Brian. He said I was flying on the last part! I said I wanted to do 2 circuits and he said that is almost the distance of Holy Isle to Lamlash. He suggested I do 1 circuit and 3 triangles and that he would support my swimming endeavours!

"Definiteness of Purpose – Clear image and vision of what we would love"
(Napoleon Hill)

28th April 2021 – Bookers Pond

I really enjoyed my swim today with Lesley and got into a good rhythm. We swam 4 diamonds. I did 1 length of front crawl, but my arms felt tired. I will need to build this up..

Chapter 7

2nd May- 29th June 2021

2nd May 2021 – Barassie Beach

Perfect morning, calm seas, so energizing. Good to practice breaststroke in the sea. Ruth took great photos and suggested using a drone next time so's I can check my stroke. Interestingly I stopped a few times as I felt the beginning of cramp even though I had porridge and a banana. I started to get cold. Ideas were flowing in my head about being authentic and how "Chatty Tuesday", my weekly podcast, really helped Ruth. Even if it only helps one person, it is of value.

3rd May 2021 – Bookers Pond

It was really cold today at only 3 degrees. Leigh and I met early at the pond and went around the small circuit 3 times. It was a chore at first but as I completed the 3rd circuit, I changed my perception and chose to relax and extend my arms instead of putting more pressure on my arms. Strangely the less effort I put in and stretched the more relaxed and comfortable I felt.

Leigh and I chatted afterwards and talked about swim events and challenges coming up. I will make sure I bring my knees up and put my feet to my bahooky to expel the water behind me and help propel me forward.

4th May 2021 – Bookers Pond

"The thought that it is only 4 months until my swim spurred me on"

I was swimming with Brian, Alison and Leigh and they went around the whole circuit whilst I decided to do one circuit and a triangle. I was thinking about how fast I was going. Slowly at first and then decided to let go. As I got to the top of the pond I relaxed, and the last stretch felt easier. I really got into the flow, even though it was quite choppy. The thought that it is only 4 months until my swim spurred me on. I will try one whole circuit and two triangles next time.

"It's not what happens to you, but how you react to it that matters"

(Epictetus)

8th May 2021 – Dunure Beach

A total impromptu swim!! At 7.15am Alex messaged me to ask if I wanted to go to Dunure for 10.00am. I agreed and was excited as I had never swum there before. I parked near the castle. We entered the water at the slipway and Alex said her stepdad would take us out on his boat to Arran in the summer and we could swim part of Holy Isle to Lamlash. Looking across to the castle was truly magical and I could also see the lighthouse on the Holy Isle quite clearly on such a beautiful sunny day. We swam to the castle and as we swam back, I felt the beginning of cramp.

An impromptu swim

9th May 2021 – Bookers Pond

It was just Cate and I initially, and we swam around the bigger circuit together. Despite being very choppy, I went around quite quickly whilst chatting away to Cate and then swam around the triangle at the end on my own.

13th May 2021 – Bookers Pond

"push my legs together faster to expel the air (and me) forward like a squid, in a ball, knees up and then a big push out"

I was finally able to get back in for a swim and decided to go around the whole circuit and did two extra smaller circuits. I felt fast today and as I swam around my breathing was perfect, totally in alignment and not out of breath. Brian suggested I focus more on my kick and push my legs together faster to expel the air (and me) forward like a squid, in a ball, knees up and then a big push out. Brian suggested I practice on a seat at home.

14th May 2021 – Bookers Pond

I was not feeling good today but was determined to try out Brian's instructions. I only did two small circuits as I had yoga straight afterwards. What a difference! Practice makes perfect! Although my breathing felt harder today.

20th May 2021 – Bookers Pond

"slow down to go faster"

It was windy today and I was the only one in the car park until Lesley arrived. I didn't have long as I didn't get in until 5.50pm and was due at my judo session at 7.00pm. I went in and it was quite choppy. I was being slapped on either side by the waves and also from the front! But I felt so alive!! As I swam to the second buoy it felt so much smoother. My goggles filled with water so I couldn't see and was reliant on the feel of the water. I completed the circuit and did a triangle. Lesley recommended gliding and my thought process was "slow down to go faster".

22nd May 2021 – Bookers Pond

A momentous swim today! Nearly a year of writing my journal and I finally managed 1600m (2 full circuits around the pond). I was focused and determined. After my first circuit I pushed on towards the top buoy. I thought I heard Leigh and Alison behind me but realised I was on my own. I asked my angels and higher power for support. I felt their presence and started to relax, my breathing slowed down, and I started to get into a comfortable rhythm. As I approached the bank, Alison was there and took a photo. Ruth also appeared and I felt elated to share my huge milestone with my swim buddies.

I finally managed 1600m!

26th May 2021 – Bookers Pond

Wow what a swim. I had not seen Janet for a while. I swam a circuit and said hi to Alison and Brian three quarters of the way around. The sun was coming out and I decided to go again. I started to feel tired as I headed up towards the top buoy. I really focused on my breathing and legs. As I got to the bank Brian high fived me! He said the only thing was that my head was too far up so prevented the flow. Everything else was great. I will try this out next time.

28th May 2021 -Bookers Pond

Eileen took a video of me swimming. I swam 1 circuit and was thinking of my swim at Greenan castle tomorrow. Trying to put all the pieces of my swim together. Stretching more, head down, more streamlined.

29th May 2021 – Greenan Castle

"I was so much faster just doing those few strokes"

I faced my fear of swimming in open water with really competent swimmers! Ruth was with me, and we joined Robert and his 2 friends Graeme and Mo, both competitive swimmers and very helpful.

Graeme came first in the Holy Isle to Lamlash splash a few times and knows it well!! His words to me were “Be respectful of the water and focus upon a target”. Robert really helped with suggestions to improve my stroke, such as putting my chest up when I breathe, go into the water flat, head down and scoop right back to my legs with my hands and feet pointing where I want to go. The sun was out, and it was lovely to swim towards Greenan shore, however, as I was so slow the 3 guys created a relay so that I was not left behind.

They all had great advice such as not bringing my chest out of the water as it acts as a barrier. As we approached the castle Robert checked that I was okay. When I said I was feeling a bit cold he said we would head back. He suggested that I should change my stroke and do front crawl as I would be faster. I explained that I was scared but tried and managed about 7 strokes before I started to panic. He said I was so much faster just doing those few strokes. The tide was quite far out so Ruth and I had quite a long walk back to get changed. We laughed, chatted until we arrived at Robert’s house, and he made us all hot chocolate.

“Be not the slave of your own past plunge into the sublime seas. Plunge deep inside yourself.”

(Ralf Waldo Emerson)

30th May 2021 – Ardeer Beach

It is one year since I started my journal! The weather today was glorious, and I went to a new location to swim. I got a bit lost but eventually met Cate, Eileen, and Lesley. We all went in and started to swim and then Alison joined us. It was so much fun as we laughed and chatted. I decided to try front crawl but realised I was swimming off to the right. I will try to correct it at the pond. I then lay on my tow float, head back and face to the sun and felt completely at peace. Once changed we had toasted marshmallows made on Eileen's basic stove.

2nd June 2021 – Bookers Pond

I was quite excited as it was my first 7.00am swim. The sun came out and I met Gilian and Alison. We did a circuit and swam breaststroke around most of the pond but for the last spurt I did front crawl. It felt good and I am challenging myself to do it tomorrow.

3rd June 2021 – Bookers Pond

“only 3 months tomorrow until my swim”

I felt very heavy and had a sore head, but I pulled myself together, had breakfast and went for a swim. I had Robert’s words in my mind about needing to swim front crawl, especially as it is only 3 months tomorrow until my Holy Isle swim. Brian and Gillian were already there, and I decided to try and do 1 small circuit of front crawl. I completed 3!! After the first one my arms were feeling heavy, like lead, but I persevered. I started to take my mind off my discomfort, taking my time in the water and focusing on my stroke. It felt much easier by the end, and I was buzzing as it felt so good.

4th June 2021 – Ballast Bank

“As we swam out towards Arran, I realised that it is only 3 months until my Holy Isle swim.

I met Brian at 8.00am. As we swam out towards Arran, I realised that it is only 3 months until my Holy Isle swim. It was very choppy today, however, so enlivening seeing the power of the waves crashing on the rocks. We swam so far beyond the rocks that my dry robe looked like a speck! We tried to take a photo of a mother duck with her ducklings with Brian’s phone, but they were too fast for us. Such a glorious swim today.

6th June 2021 – Portencross

As Lesley, Eileen and I entered the water at the castle I had not realized Little Cumbrae was so far away. As I swam front crawl, it was amazing to see all the wildlife beneath the sea. Looking up I could see Holy Isle to my left and realised I was swimming in the same water. As I swam back towards the castle, with the blue sky behind, it looked so magical. Upon exiting I had the notion of going back in without my gloves and pulled the top part of my wetsuit down. I laughed so much with my swim buddies as it was cold, such heart-warming camaraderie.

Portencross

7th June 2021 – Bookers Pond

"chin to chest, look down and under your 'Oxters'

Brian swam alongside me this morning, for the whole circuit of the pond and gave me lots of guidance. He mentioned ... "chin to chest, look down and under your 'Oxters' (armpits) to breathe and slow the stroke down so that you can feel it and do not go like a steamroller"! I tried to breathe to both sides but kept swallowing water (it did not feel natural). I learnt so much today and loved my swim.

8th June 2021 – Bookers Pond

The sun came out today as I entered the water. Lesley suggested we do 2 small circuits. I did front crawl and did not stop for the whole time. I tried to make sure I was not crossing my arms over the Centre line as I was a bit all over the place. However, despite this, Lesley said she had to speed up to catch up with me. I was feeling faster today.

9th June 2021 – Bookers Pond

"developing muscle memory"

Brian and I swam the circuit together this morning. I started well then felt my arms go heavy and was going off course. Brian talked about not crossing my left arm over the centre line whilst swimming, as this is what would send me off course. I kept trying and realised I was going too fast, so I slowed down, lengthening my arms which helped me go faster and remain more aligned. Brian said this was about developing muscle memory. I need to change my limiting mindset in order to develop the correct muscle memory and stop me falling back into old and poorer habits.

10th June 2021 – Bookers Pond

I was determined to work harder and iron out my errors today. Brian followed me and we stopped at the top end of the pond. I was still crossing my left arm over the centre line and going off course. Brian suggested tucking my chin into my chest and I did slightly better, but still need to work on this.

11th June 2021 – Bookers Pond

I saw Gillian in the distance and was determined to do a circuit whilst trying to put Brian's advice into practice. My arms felt heavy on the first stretch, but I let this go. I was completely on my own as I reached the top of the pond. It was both scary and exhilarating at the same time. I could still feel myself veering off but self-corrected. I did my live video as it felt good to not have any stops.

12th June 2021 – Bookers Pond

"I swam over 2000 metres!!"

I was so happy as I met Lesley at 7.30am (no peace for the wicked!!!). I did a circuit and felt a bit crampy towards the end but decided to do a second. Lesley was doing the same and we pushed each other on (the benefit of having swim buddies). I felt cramp a few times but said to myself "mind over matter". I was feeling tired once I reached the top and asked my "angels" to help and had a real sense of them replying "believe, trust and focus". I really focused on my stroke and my left arm especially and was more aligned. I felt much calmer. "Relax and go with the flow" was what was going through my mind! I swam over 2000 metres!! I was so happy.

13th June 2021 – Bookers Pond

It was lovely to be met by Ruth in the car park. Brian was also present, and I did one full circuit. My focus was totally on my alignment. I did drift slightly but was able to pull it back. As I did my second circuit, I was getting frustrated with myself, realizing that I was going off course. I tried to bring myself back in alignment then lost my rhythm and started to get cramp. This happened at the Pacman also when I went around in circles. I relayed my feelings to Brian, and he advised me to attempt to bring my right arm over the centre line. That did help to correct my alignment. Something "clicked", and my arms were able to massively help me steer. As I watched Diane Nyad's journey (she is a well renowned long-distance swimmer and motivational speaker) it really resonated with me, and I appreciated the importance of resilience and a strong mindset.

"I am overwhelmed by the strength of my body and the power of my mind. For one moment, just one second, I feel immortal."

(Diana Nyad)

14th June 2021 – Bookers Pond

I met Brian at the pond and the focus was on my breathing. He spoke about muscle memory and getting out of old negative patterns. He reminded me to use my right arm slightly over the centre line and I started going in a straighter line and was more easily able to self-correct, especially at the top buoys in the pond.

15th June 2021 – Bookers Pond

Wow!! Lots of insights today. I really focused on all of Brian's teachings, and it was starting to come together. I was so much straighter although I did bang into the bottom Pacman buoy but still shaved 10 minutes off my previous best time!!

16th June 2021 – Bookers Pond

"how to breathe "bubbles"

Brian swam around with me today to help me stay more in alignment. It was the first time I reached the top buoy in a straight line. Brian stopped me at the last buoy and said I was breathing "explosively" and would not be able to sustain this.

He showed me how to breathe "bubbles", hold my breath and gently breathe in. Wow what a difference!! I felt much more relaxed by the end of my swim. Brian applauded the difference, commenting that this would help me to stay strong and not get so tired.

17th June 2021 – Bookers Pond

Brian was at the pond with Gillian, so I went around on my own. I really focused on my breathing, and it seemed to go a lot better. I was off course slightly but easily rectified things. Blowing bubbles is key!

18th June 2021 – Bookers Pond & Portencross

I was on my own today. I imagined that Brian and Gillian were there and felt fine. I stayed reasonably focused. After the last triangle I realised that I could, in fact, have easily kept going but decided to call it a day as I was the only person at the pond. Eileen suggested a swim at Portencross with marshmallows later that day. Max came with me and gave it 11 out of 10!!! It was a real test for me as the water was quite choppy. I kept getting water in my mouth. So, I focused on front crawl instead of breaststroke and did ok!

Max gave Portencross 11 out of 10!!!

19th June 2021 – Irvine Beach

I met Eileen and Swam out towards the "Stone Dragon" (a landmark on the hillside). On the way back I swam non-stop and got into a nice rhythm. I was close to the shore and could see the seabed beneath me which was very calming.

20th June 2021 – Bookers Pond

My 16th day in a row!! It was so lovely to see Ruth today. I wanted to go around the pond two times. As I did my second circuit and was going towards the top buoy, I started to get a bit disorientated and was feeling tired but recalibrated my breathing and tried to focus on good alignment. I managed the two circuits and one triangle, about 1.8K in total!

21st June 2021 – Bookers Pond

(Summer Solstice!!)

I was the only one on the pond this morning and the sun was just rising as I just “went for it”!! I managed to go all the way around without veering off course! I did not end up in the reeds! Surprising!! It was all down to breathing and focus.

22nd June 2021 – Bookers Pond

I arrived slightly later today and saw Gillian and Jill in the distance as I approached the bank. Jill (another lifeguard!!) offered me tips to improve my technique. I started going around, focusing on my breathing, alignment and relaxing and managed to stay straight and not go into the reeds. I started to feel more “at one” with the water. Having the sun beating down on me was glorious.

“Be the change you want to be”

(Anon)

23rd June 2021 – Bookers Pond

"I felt great that I pushed myself through the negative mindset"

I arrived at 7.15am and the pond was deserted! I decided to do three circuits of the triangle to practice breathing/alignment and did very well, shaving five minutes off my time. I realized that three times around is 900 metres and not 750 metres as I had previously been told!! Lesson for the day – even though I didn't feel up to going in awful weather I felt great that I pushed myself through the negative mindset.

24th June 2021 – Bookers Pond

(21 days in a row!!)

I started on my own at the pond. I felt good that I was out in the sun and swimming. I enjoyed swimming around today and felt right "on track"! This will be my last swim for a few days. As I got out of the pond a lady, I had seen a few times previously at the pond said to me "21". She remembered that I was attempting to swim 21 days in a row!! Such a great achievement.

29th June 2021 – Bookers Pond

I was so happy to be back in the water after 5 days away!! I was desperate to get back in! As I started swimming, I was gliding and consciously slowing down towards the second buoy. Brian commented on how straight I was which made me feel very pleased with myself. I got slight cramp on the long stretch towards the bottom buoy because I got scared when I saw the reeds. Almost immediately my feet went into cramp which I overcame after a few minutes focusing on my positive mindset. Brian got out of the pond and “high-fived” me! He couldn’t find fault and I shaved a few minutes off my time! Brian (knowing I was going over to Lamlash) suggested going to the end of the houses in Lamlash as there are fewer reeds. I will try this when I’m over there on Thursday. This will be good “acclimatisation” as my big swim will be Lamlash to Holy Isle and back.

Chapter 8

1st July – 31st August 2021

1st July 2021 – Lamlash Bay

"it was amazing to finally be in the actual water where my charity swim will take place"

Wow!! Here I am in Lamlash and last night I looked out from the ramp at my swimming route. I got ready today and Max was with me. I walked out into the sea, and it was amazing to finally be in the actual water where my charity swim will take place. I swam out a bit but there were lots of reeds and seaweed. As I approached the church in Lamlash Bay I encountered what I thought were jellyfish with a long thin, white, reedy appearance. I was flat on the water and decided to change direction and head back. As I swam back Holy Isle was on my right (breathing) side and I felt at one with the water and closer to my goal. I didn't want to get out!! My stroke was really flowing, and I felt good.

Finally swimming in the waters at Lamlash

3rd July 2021 – Bookers Pond

I met Brian at the pond today and he was really supportive on my third circuit. He said he would time me to see how I was progressing. Three times around the smaller circuits and I was feeling tired. It felt good even though I coughed up quite a lot of water. I managed it in 19 minutes. I was delighted. Brian asked if I was going to go around a fourth time, but I declined.

4th July 2021 – Bookers Pond

"I was conscious that it is only 2 months today that I do my Holy Isle swim!"

I met Ruth for a swim today and she made us both put up four fingers and say "four"!! As I went in, I started to swim straight away, and it felt good, but I was veering off to the right to begin with. I completed three circuits and thought I would go for a fourth as I was conscious that it is only 1 month today that I do my Holy Isle swim! It was great and I really got into my rhythm (almost 3K)! I was so delighted that I managed four!

5th July 2021 – Bookers Pond

I was in two minds today about whether to go into the pond because it was raining, but once I was in it was so energizing. I kept veering to the right so was always trying to self-correct. I decided to do two circuits today after my lengthy swim yesterday. By the second time around I felt in much better alignment and at peace in the pond.

7th July 2021 – Bookers Pond

"the first time I managed to swim in a completely straight line to the top buoy"

Today I was back at 7.00am. I timed myself and went in at 7.28am and came out at 8.12am. It was the first time I managed to swim in a completely straight line to the top buoy. I realised that it takes me a while to get into my flow on the first lap. The second length was much easier and by the final length before the Pacman I felt as though I was watching the trees go by and starting to swim on automatic as if I was driving my car and not focusing on my arms. The sun was shining today which really helped me feel alive.

8th July 2021 – Irvine Beach

"I need to ride the waves rather than fight them"

Finally, back in the sea after a week (this time last week I was in Lamlash Bay!). I met Eileen and went into the water. I was determined to swim front crawl to the stone dragon and back. It felt very different to Bookers as it was so choppy. As I headed out to the stone dragon, I got into a good rhythm but realised upon looking up that I was very far to the right so adjusted and made it past the stone dragon and began to swim back.

As I did so the waves had clearly changed and I was having to work really hard to overcome the push of the waves. That's when I realized, I need to ride the waves rather than fight them. As I let the waves rock my body, I was then able to move through and with the waves much faster! I was so "in the zone" that I bumped into Eileen. I stopped to chat, and we laughed and began to relax before turning back for the shore. I got changed and sat on a bench which looked out to sea. The camaraderie was amazing, chatting away whilst snugly wrapped in my dry robe.

9th July 2021 – Bookers Pond

I double dipped today. Bookers both times. I went in first at 7.00am and I saw Brian finishing the last part of the Pacman. I decided to go do my circuit as I knew he would soon catch up. I tried to stay focused and once at the top managed to get into a good rhythm. I finished the Pacman and saw Brian just completing his Pacman. He said he couldn't catch up with me and that my time was much faster (really whizzing around the top of the circuit in his words!!). I only managed one circuit this morning. I went back to Bookers at 4.30pm and it was very busy. It was great to swim with Cate, Lesley and Eileen and just have a gentle swim with them.

If a man does not keep pace with his companions, perhaps it is because he hears a different drummer. Let him step to the music which he hears, however measured or far away"
(Henry David Thoreau)

10th July 2021 – Croy Shore

I was picked up by Eileen and we went to Croy Shore for an evening swim. Cate and Alex joined us. The sunset was stunning and such an enjoyable swim, heading towards the crab nets. As we turned back to the shore, I could hear a guitar strumming and there were little camp fire lights all along the shoreline. Once on land Eileen set up a fire and made toasted marshmallows. Max sat in a chair, in his element. What a perfect night.

A perfect night for relaxing

11th July 2021 – Bookers Pond

A frustrating swim, the pond was full of paddle boarders as it was 5.00pm but I was determined to go. As I got to the top buoy there were about four paddle boarders having a lesson and I had to do a big loop to get around them then I briefly lost my goggles, which I think slipped off my head as I was wearing two swim hats!! I swam to the next buoy and then put one swim hat back on and tucked the other into my wet suit and put my goggles back on. I met a few more paddle boarders heading towards me and quickly decided I wouldn't swim at 5.00pm again!!

12th July 2021 – Bookers Pond

Lovely and quiet and I managed four times around the pond. My first circuit felt good but slow. On my second circuit I had cramp but continued. On my third circuit I felt quite tired but felt perfect by the fourth circuit!

14th July 2021 – Bookers Pond

Great swim! Three times around as the sun rose and it felt so energizing. I was, however, going off course but quickly managed to right myself and felt in better alignment as I was finishing my swim.

15th July 2021 – Bookers Pond

There was bright sunshine this morning and I managed to stay well aligned until the top buoy and noticed the reeds and moss at the top of the pond but managed to keep on track. By the third lap I was fairly flying around and knocked five minutes off my time! I really got into my rhythm.

Keeping on track at Bookers

20th July 2021 – The Cotswolds

Here I am at the lakes of the Cotswolds!! I went kayaking and felt very tense and slightly scared, so I moved to the back of the kayak and Max steered it from the front. This felt so much better, but I decided to swim back from the far side and decided that I would stick to swimming rather than kayaking!! It felt quite surreal swimming in the water where I had just kayaked!! I was heading towards an island and as I approached, I got caught in the pond weed. This was quite scary, but I managed to calm down and avoid getting into a panic. As I swam back to the jetty, I needed to be helped up by some people there as the water was very “mulchy”. My feet and swim shoes were covered in silt.

21st July 2021 – The Cotswolds

I was back in the big lake today with Ann-Marie and Daniel, my sister in law and her son Daniel offering kayak support. This time I swam around two smaller islands. I got into a great rhythm but nearing the second island was so shallow I could stand up. I persevered and it turned out to be a magical morning with the sun shining through the trees.

A first swim in the lakes

22nd July 2021 – Cotswolds swimming pool!!

"My first-time swimming lengths of front crawl in a swimming pool since I was 18!!"

This was my first-time swimming lengths of front crawl in a swimming pool since I was 18!! It was strange to feel my fingers and toes (no gloves or swim shoes!) so it took a while to adjust to the heat. I did 40 lengths.

23rd July 2021 – Still in the Cotswolds!!

What a beautiful lake Ann-Marie took me to! We needed to cycle for about 15 minutes to get there but it was so worth it!! I swam from one side of the lake to the other. It was a bit disorientating on the way back as I couldn't see Ann-Marie on the bank. I swam backwards and forwards a few times over about 45 minutes. It was so peaceful.

24th July 2021 – Cotswold Swimming Pool

Back in the pool today. I was more "in the zone" and used the pool floor markers to guide me and keep me aligned. I did 70 lengths and it felt really good.

27th July 2021 – Bookers Pond

Back to Bookers. I only did two circuits today, but it felt incredible to be back. It was lovely to see the familiar orange buoy that Brian had placed at the pond with all the "Aquaducks" names thereon, including mine!

28th July 2021 – Bookers Pond

I needed my swim this morning! I had the pond to myself. I was so “in the zone”, thinking through my work presentation, that I spent 1hour & 45 minutes in the pond. I was late for an appointment with my accountant as a result!!

30th July 201 – Bookers Pond

It was lovely to see Brian, Alison, and Cate today. I was very focused and swimming quite straight although my neck felt sore on the way out where my wetsuit had been rubbing! I met Peter, who is funny, good company and a great swimmer. He said he had been swimming at Bookers for about three months.

31st July 2021 – Ballast Bank

I was very excited today a I went to the bank with Cate. Paul, who runs the group, was there. He was so friendly and provided many tips. It felt quite cold, and we swam to the rocks and back about five times and then around the larger rock and back to the shore.

I was blown away when Cate gave me a jasper necklace made with stones from the beach! It was so beautiful. It felt so incredible sitting by the rock, looking out towards Holy Isle with the sun shining down creating beautiful pathways on the water's surface.

Pathways of light at Ballast Bank

1st August 2021 – Irvine Beach

"in the zone"

I met Eileen at Irvine car park. Max was with me, and he wore my wetsuit as his was too tight and he used Eileen's float. I need to get another float. Max said it was cold as we all swam together for a bit. Eileen asked if I wanted to do a solo swim. I swam to the stone dragon and back and felt so "in the zone" and felt I could have swum for miles. As I swam back from the stone dragon, I became aware of the sandy seabed as I totally relaxed so I heard the words symbiotic/symbiosis and I felt that connection or "oneness" with nature.

2nd August 2021 – Bookers Pond

I went for a later swim today (midday). I did two circuits of the pond, and the second circuit was crazy busy with paddle boarders. I will need to make sure I come early tomorrow. As I left the pond the sky was blue, and it was warm. I got talking to another swimmer who had completed a half "Iron man" and Holy Isle to Lamlash as part of that and said it was about 2.5 Pac-mans.

3rd August 2021 – Bookers Pond

"I knew I had to push myself to go as it is a month today that I do my Holy Isle swim"

Wow, what a swim!! I was not in the mood at all today as it was pouring down, but I knew I had to push myself to go as it is a month today that I do my Holy Isle swim. I entered at 8.30am and the pond was dead. I was the only one there. I started going around and veered off to the right and focused my attention on realigning myself. I saw some fishermen on the right-side bank as I was swimming down. After three smaller circuits I was in my flow and decided to try five. I wasn't out of breath. On my fifth lap I was totally relaxed and again heard the word symbiosis.

This time it made sense as I was at one with the water and vice versa. It was such a powerful experience, I felt I was simply gliding around the pond. I felt so proud as I finished up, however on getting out of the water I realised my neck was sore and discovered a massive friction burn on the right side of my neck due, I suspect, to me always breathing to the right. My swim buddy, Alison said she had the same thing after three circuits of the pond in her wetsuit.

6th August 2021 – Bookers Pond

"persistence"

I was excited but slightly apprehensive about going into the pond today as my alarm awoke me at 6.20am. I was tempted, upon hearing the rain outside, just to roll over in my bed – but no! I was determined I was going in!! I got to the pond for 7.15am and swam for about an hour doing two circuits and a triangle today, the equivalent of Holy Isle to Lamlash and visualized this as I was swimming around. During my swim I kept hearing the word "persistence" then, when in my car, I listened to Bob Proctor (a motivational speaker) talking about "Persistence" – a definite theme!

7th August 2021 – Bookers Pond

I went into the pond for 9.00am today and saw two robes, thinking it might have been Brian and Alison, but they belonged to two ladies. I met Peter again on my way out of the water and then heard a scream and Ruth's voice calling out "CC!" (her nickname for me!). she said, "CC so lovely to see you" and that was so strange as I had been thinking about her the night before. Ruth and I decided to do four circuits today and I set off slightly before her as I was sure she would quickly catch up with me, but she didn't and stayed behind me the whole way. I felt great as I was very fluid, especially on the way down the pond and again I stayed totally in alignment with my breathing remaining very calm.

8th August 2021 – Grey Mares Tail

I was so excited. I drove to Cate's with Max. Alex joined us as we travelled in the back of Cate's car. 1.5 hours later we were sitting at the bottom of the Grey Mares Tail. As I started to climb up I got a pain in my chest, tightness and difficulty in breathing. I had to really take my time and relax. One step at a time! I reached the top passing the waterfall which is the "Grey Mares Tail" and saw the stunning view of the lochan. I gently eased myself into the water as it was very rocky.

I swam out to join my swim buddies on the other side of the lochan and then swam back to get Max, then the two of us swam to the island in the middle of the lochan with the tree on it. As we headed back down the path it was raining torrentially. I realised I had wet feet and was slipping and needed to invest in new walking shoes. My toe-float, resting against my belly helped to keep me a bit drier. I was the last to get off the hill as I kept sliding on my bum on the way down!!

Climbing to have a lofty swim with Max

9th August 2021 – Bookers Pond

I arrived at 9.00am and really didn't feel like going in as I was so tired from yesterday and the rain was still teeming down. I was the only person there (again) and did two circuits, the second of which felt really smooth. It turned out to be such a relaxing, peaceful swim.

11th August 2021 – Bookers Pond

I did not get in today until 8.30am, however I decided to keep going. I met two regular pond swimmers (as they whizzed past me!). I did two circuits in their wake before catching up with them. I could feel the ease in my stroke today especially down the end straight to the bottom buoy. I decided to continue and ended up completing four circuits!!

12th August 2021 – Bookers Pond

I met Brian at the pond at 6.50am. He was already in the water and we breast-stroked to the second buoy, chatting about my challenge and his health. We did two circuits and then left. As we were changing Brian said he would bring his kayak over to accompany me on my Holy Isle challenge. I was keen on doing my challenge on the 4th of September. As we were talking Jill approached. She had just completed a "Channel Swim Relay" challenge and said she would be happy to swim with me and donate to my charity (Mental Health Foundation).

"The quality of persistence is to the character of man, what carbon is to steel"

(Napoleon Hill)

13th August 2021 – Bookers Pond

It was bucketing down today as I headed up to the second buoy. I was being buffeted by my toe-float and the currents. I made it to the top buoy where it was slightly less windy and kept telling myself to persist. I was tempted not to go in today but challenged myself as I will be in the sea, and it may well be choppy for my Holy Isle swim and was thinking that this would be good practice. I did a circuit and a triangle and felt good.

14th August 2021 – Bookers Pond

"I swam two circuits and a triangle (the equivalent of Holy Isle to Lamlash)"

I met with Alex at 10.30am today. She was with her step-sister, and they went around the pond once as her step-sister was practicing for a Loch Lomond swim. I swam two circuits and a triangle (the equivalent of Holy Isle to Lamlash) and as I came out Alex took a video of me to promote my swim for charity. I had been listening to Bob Proctor who was telling us to "build a fire under our desire".

15th August 2021 – Bookers Pond

It was lovely to see Lesley and Eileen today. Lesley was a great marker for my circuit and made me go faster. Initially I was expending more effort through my arms but slowly started to lengthen and gently find my rhythm. I will try to get my Orca suit fixed as it has greater flexibility under the arms. I did two and a half circuits.

16th August 2021 – Bookers Pond

"to stay within my imaginary "box"

It was quiet at the pond this morning and felt very cold. The first length was slightly slower than my second when I started, not moving my arms outside the "box" to become more streamlined. I was trying to stay within my imaginary "box" to stay tight, streamlined and more efficient.

"The starting point of what we want to achieve is desire, Building a fire under your desire"

(Napoleon Hill)

25th August 2021 – Double dip day

(Bookers Pond and then Irvine Beach)

I was at the pond first this morning and bumped into Gillian. She mentioned she was doing the "Polar Bear" challenge. I did two circuits and a triangle. On my way out I met two men who had actually swam Holy Isle to Lamlash. They both said that it was easier to swim Holy Isle to Lamlash (than the pond) due to the buoyancy the salty seawater provided. Eileen invited me to swim at Irvine Beach later in the day. That was the first time in a while I had been to the beach. It was quite choppy but good to practice my breathing. Eileen then came to my house to help repair my wetsuit.

26th August 2021 – Bookers Pond

"It was as though he was "sent" to help at that time!!"

I entered the pond at 7.00am, swimming two circuits and a triangle. I was very happy with my pace. Brian and Janet were waiting at the bank. Brian asked how I felt I had done, and I said I was happy with the swim in 45 minutes. He said my arms were all wrong and that I needed to stretch them out more. He advised that my arms should brush against my ears. The way I was stretching was causing more resistance as my elbow was too bent. It was as though he was "sent" to help at that time!!

27th August 2021 – Double dip day again

(Bookers Pond and Irvine Beach)

My alarm went off at 5.45am this morning!! I was determined, if a bit apprehensive, to practice my new stroke based upon Brian's advice. It seemed very tiring at first but after one full circuit I was becoming more comfortable with it. I realised that I had been using Brian's stroke advice more when I was near the reeds as I had to swim slower near them. I heard the phrase "slow down to go faster" and was whizzing around the full straight, my heart racing, and finished in 43 minutes! This evening at 4.45pm I then met Eileen at Irvine Beach. Max also came and loved seeing the various sea life with his snorkel.

I swam to the cross. Eileen reckoned it was about one kilometre out and that it could be dangerous, so I made sure to stay well to the left of it. I managed to get there quite easily and when I came back Eileen said she briefly lost sight of me but then picked me up again and felt I would have no problems swimming from Holy Isle to Lamlash. She took a video and posted it on social media for other people to see what I was doing. 10 days to go!!!

Training for The Swim

28th August 2021 – Irvine Beach

"mind over matter"

A lie in – woohoo!! I felt I needed a rest then met Lesley and Eileen at 5.00pm and we swam for about 45 minutes. Lesley said she had seen some Lion's Mane jellyfish. Luckily, I didn't!! I swam to the cross and back where it was quite choppy and required a "mind over matter" approach. At points I felt I wasn't moving at all!! Max loved his snorkel mask and was able to go flat and explore the depths, crabs and fish.

29th August 2021 – Bookers Pond

I agreed to meet Eileen and Lesley today at 9.30am. On the way I met a couple of swimmers I used to see quite regularly in the mornings and said that my challenge swim was the following Sunday and they donated £20!! I started swimming but felt very constricted in my wetsuit and nearly bumped into Lesley as I reached the Pac man. We chatted and I did the breaststroke to the final buoy. I then swam around again, and I felt so much freer and swam at a really good pace.I reflected with Lesley afterwards that perhaps the breaststroke had stretched my muscles out and that I would try to do stretches before my next swim.

30th August 2021 – Irvine Beach

"It was all worth it. Robin was willing me on"

I was feeling quite tired this evening after a very busy day at work. I met Eileen and we went into a slightly chilly sea. I felt my wetsuit fill up and as I started swimming, so my face began to feel numb. I pushed through this. My rhythm was poor, but I got to the cross losing my sense of direction a few times.

I swam past the cross and looked out towards Holy Isle and said to myself "I will be with you on Sunday"!! as I did so the clouds parted and there were streaky rays of sunshine through the clouds and onto Holy Isle. I felt those rays and they energized me. I swam back twice as fast and was flowing well and feeling that it was all worth it and Robin was willing me on.

"You can't control everything. Sometimes you just need to relax and have faith that things will work out... Let go a little and just let life happen"

(Kody Keplinger)

31st August 2021 – Bookers Pond

I didn't get into the pond until 7.20am so I only had time to do one circuit. I had the pond to myself and sped around it, completing my swim in 18 minutes. My focus was the Holy Isle swim, seeing the faces of people as I reached the finishing line.

Chapter 9

1st – 4th September 2021

1st September 2021 – Bookers Pond

"Only 4 days to go!!"

I had a lovely swim at Bookers. The sun was shining down beautifully, and I could feel the warmth on my back. I got into a good rhythm and knew I was going to manage two circuits this morning which I did in 37 minutes!! Eileen asked if I wanted to go to Irvine Beach later and I took Max, but it was a bumpy swim. I kept getting water in my goggles and became disorientated as a result. I was really pushing against the waves.On the way back it was easier as the waves were pushing me forward. I managed to build some momentum, but the current was strong. I relaxed with it and managed to get back into the zone. Only 4 days to go!!

2nd September 2021 – Bookers Pond

"The enormity of my swim challenge was finally dawning on me!"

As I walked along the path towards the pond, I started feeling slightly nervous. The enormity of my swim challenge was finally dawning on me! I felt the cold enter my body as I entered the water. The hole in my wetsuit will need repairing. Eileen said she would help. As I swam around the pond, I was attempting to fully extend my arms, thinking of all the things Brian and Robert had taught me. I really got into the zone and did my two circuits in 38 minutes.

3rd September 2021 – Bookers Pond

"I felt Robin and Heather with me, in spirit, today"

The last day at the pond before my swim challenge!! I was feeling really excited today and remembered when I first recorded myself going into the pond on October 31st last year and saying that I wanted to achieve my goal within a year and here I am!! Who could have known all that would happen! As I swam today, I felt a bit slow as I was wearing my old wetsuit, however I managed my two circuits. I met Billy and Eddie (they are the guys who did the half iron man the previous year) again. They echoed that I was more buoyant and protected in the sea. I felt Robin and Heather (my pupil) with me, in spirit, today as I swam around the pond. I'm feeling very excited about tomorrow and that, as of now, I have raised £926!

4th September 2021 – TODAY'S THE DAY!!

I awoke feeling anxious and excited with butterflies in my stomach. I have been working for so long to achieve my dream and it's finally here!! I met Ian, a family friend and June, his wife, with her niece Ashley and her son Andrew, at the ferry. As Brian and I arrived in Lamlash we met Margaret and Iain, my boat support crew, at the jetty. Brian and I got changed in the yacht club. Brian set off towards Holy Isle and Max and I followed in the support boat.

As Brian reached Holy Isle I met him on the jetty and reflected that three years ago I came to Holy Isle on a course and found what I believe to be my "spiritual sanctuary" and here I am thinking "this is it!!" I climbed down the steps, met Brian in the water and off we went! I tried to calm my mind and relax. I followed Brian but couldn't really see my line of sight very well. I had a huge sense of peace, awe and wonder at being surrounded by the vastness of the sea. Conditions were perfect for swimming, and I had an overwhelming sense of freedom and space. As I got half-way across my left leg froze and my foot was stuck in a strange position.

It wasn't cramp! I really had to concentrate and refocus my mind and work on my breathing. After a further fifteen minutes the sensation in my leg subsided and I then spotted some jellyfish. Brian informed me that I had already kicked a few away!! I passed a green marker I had seen on the way over on the boat. I then noticed lots of small yachts and the jetty with all the white mental health T-shirts and started to really appreciate the enormity of what I was doing and took my time on the ramp trying to compose myself before getting out of the water. As I did so everyone started to cheer, and I felt really emotional.

I had done it for Robin, myself and my boys!! I got changed and went to eat something in the nearby restaurant where I was given £30 in donations from the staff who saw our T-shirts and heard my story. As I got back onto the ferry there was a tannoy announcement from the captain announcing my swim achievement!! Everyone in the boat was cheering as the tears rolled down my cheeks!! THE END!!

My swim team on the day

What's Next

The story you have just read was the beginning of my open water swim journey in 2020/2021. It taught me many lessons about overcoming obstacles, pushing through fear and navigating the waves of grief and the sea.

My story emphasises the fact that I am just an ordinary swimmer with no competitive training. I have always enjoyed being in the water and I found a way to use this hobby to raise money for charities that are close to my heart. My wish to help those struggling with their mental health and addiction has given me the opportunity to meet some amazing individuals and create lifelong friendships. I am truly grateful!

I am planning on writing a book about the incredible journey my charity swimming has taken me on since 2021 such as; lessons learnt, tools and insights I have uncovered. I will keep you updated on my website ***www.SoulsLightSolutions*** for all my upcoming swim events and future book releases.

Whatever your thought, dream or goal (no matter how crazy it might seem) I hope my story has given you the belief and inspiration to GO FOR IT!

Acknowledgements

Alex, Alison, Anne-Marie, Billy M, Billy and Eddie, Brian, Cate, Chris, Eileen, Frances, Gillian, Graeme/Mo, Janet, Jill, Katie, Ken, Leigh, Lesley, Linda, Margaret/Iain, Max, Paul, Peter, Rachel, Robin S and Ruth, Kat.

Thank you for being part of my circle of support.

Whilst I am immensely proud of my own growth and achievements over the course of this amazing journey, raising over £1500 for Mental Health Foundation, I am reminded of the words of one of my all-time heroines, Diane Nyad. Upon reaching the Floridian beach she said that she could not have achieved her great feat alone and that she had learned the value of 'team' in achieving her ambition.

The names in the above circle constitute most of the team involved, at various stages, of my swim journey. I have kept it simple. They know who they are and how much they've meant to me. Without their help, support and guidance, I would still be meandering my way up and down Prestwick swimming pool doing length after length of breast stroke!!

Each one of you has been an integral part of my journey. Your support, guidance, friendship, and belief helped me to grow and turn my dream into reality.

Wild Swimming Tips

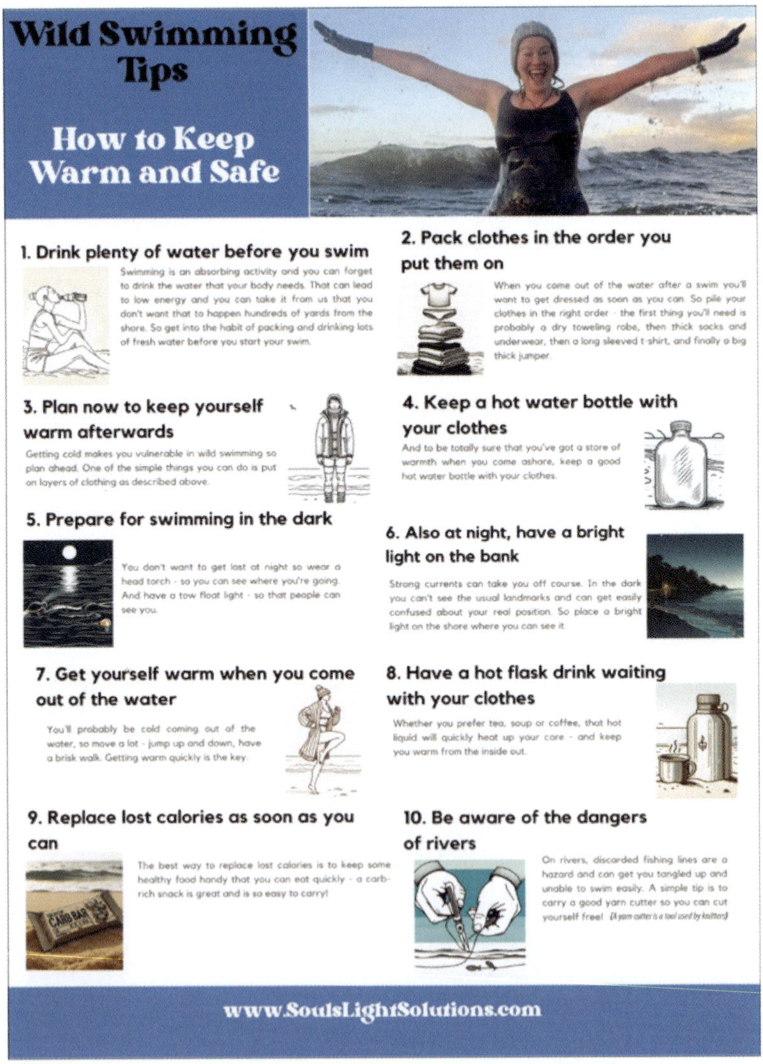

Printed in Poland
by Amazon Fulfillment
Poland Sp. z o.o., Wrocław

34543180R00078